Bernd Teufel

Organization of Programming Languages

Springer-Verlag   Wien New York

Dr. Bernd Teufel
FAW Ulm, Bereich Büroautomation
Federal Republic of Germany

© 1991 by Springer-Verlag/Wien

Printed on acid-free paper

With 50 Figures

ISBN-13: 978-3-211-82315-6   e-ISBN-13: 978-3-7091-9186-6
DOI: 10.1007/978-3-7091-9186-6

Preface

Beside the computers itself, programming languages are the most important tools of a computer scientist, because they allow the formulation of algorithms in a way that a computer can perform the desired actions. Without the availability of (high level) languages it would simply be impossible to solve complex problems by using computers. Therefore, high level programming languages form a central topic in Computer Science. It should be a must for every student of Computer Science to take a course on the organization and structure of programming languages, since the knowledge about the design of the various programming languages as well as the understanding of certain compilation techniques can support the decision to choose the right language for a particular problem or application.

This book is about high level programming languages. It deals with all the major aspects of programming languages (including a lot of examples and exercises). Therefore, the book does not give an detailed introduction to a certain programming language (for this it is referred to the original language reports), but it explains the most important features of certain programming languages using those programming languages to exemplify the problems. The book was outlined for a one session course on programming languages. It can be used both as a teacher's reference as well as a student text book.

Chapter One gives an introductory overview of programming languages. The evolution of programming languages is shown and the views of three outstanding Computer Scientists, Backus, Hoare, and Wirth, whose work is closely related with the definition, design, and development of programming languages, are given. The basic terminology and elements for language description are introduced.

Chapter Two is about language processing. Syntax and semantics, formal languages and grammars are introduced as well as compiler aspects and run-time environments. These are the fundamental aspects which are important for the understanding of certain problems of programming languages.

Chapter Three deals with data types. The concept of binding is discussed followed by an introductory to elementary data types, structured data types, as well as abstract data types. Problems of type checking and the implementation of data types are outlined. Finally variables - the carriers of certain types - are considered in terms of scope and lifetime.

Chapter Four introduces expressions and control structures in programming languages. While expressions specify how values have to be calculated, control structures allow the programmer to define the order of execution of statements. The distinction between implicit and explicit control structures is introduced, followed by a discussion of control structures on statement level and on the level of program units.

Chapter Five is about procedures. While procedures were already introduced in Chapter Four as an instrument to manipulate the flow of control in a program system, in Chapter Five procedures are discussed in terms of parameter passing, overloading, and generic concepts, as well as implementation techniques. However, the Chapter starts with a brief overview of the basic ideas behind procedures.

Chapter Six deals with data encapsulation. The basic ideas of data encapsulation (and, thus, of abstract data types) are introduced. Concepts of abstraction, information hiding, and encapsulation are considered before certain abstraction techniques in SIMULA 67, C++, EIFFEL, MODULA-2, and ADA are discussed.

Chapter Seven considers the concept of inheritance in programming languages. inheritance means the definition of new entities on the basis of existing ones and that those new entities inherit the properties of the existing ones. Besides a brief discussion about subranges in PASCAL and MODULA-2 and subtypes in ADA, the concept of type extension in OBERON is introduced. Thereafter, inheritance in SIMULA 67, SMALLTALK, and C++ is discussed. It is shown that inheritance does not work in the same way in these languages.

Chapter Eight discusses the concepts of concurrency and appropriate features in programming languages. Coroutines in SIMULA 67 are introduced as an example of quasi-parallelism. Thereafter, concurrent units which are used to satisfy a common goal are considered. Such units need to communicate to each other and they need to be synchronized. Thus, appropriate methods, such as shared variables, semaphores, monitors, and messages, are discussed. The Chapter is concluded by an example of concurrency in ADA.

Chapter Nine introduces briefly the three major approaches in the description of semantics in programming languages. these approaches are: Operational semantics, denotational semantics, and axiomatic semantics. The first method introduces a virtual computer to describe the meaning of basic language concepts, while the others represent a mathematical way of description.

A great number of *Exercises* is separately included to allow the reader to assess his understanding of the book`s content.

Acknowledgements

I am deeply indebted to a number of individuals who have made valuable suggestions about the content and form of this material, especially Dr. Stephanie Schmidt of the University of Zürich, Switzerland, who supported and assisted me in writing this book. I thank a number of students of my course on the *Organization of Programming Languages* at the University of Wollongong (UoW), Australia, for their critical discussions. I am also most grateful to Dr. Peter Nickolas of UoW, who gave me a lot of valuable hints for the preparation of my course on Programming Languages. Special thanks are due to Professor Greg Doherty, the Head of Department of Computer Science at UoW, and Dr. Fritz Hille of the Swiss Federal Institute of Technology (ETH), for having made possible a sabbatical year in Wollongong in 1989-90 when I wrote this book. I thank all these individuals for their guidance and assistance.

Pfaffenhofen an der Roth, 1991

Bernd Teufel

Contents

1 Principles of Programming Languages

A *programming language* is a systematic notation by which computational processes are described [HORO 84]. Beside the computers itself, programming languages are the most important tools of a computer scientist, because they allow the formulation of algorithms in a way that a computer can perform the desired actions. Without the availability of (high level) languages it would simply be impossible to solve complex problems by using computers, since they understand just binary instructions. Therefore, it should be a must for every student of Computer Science to take a course on the organization and structure of programming languages.

This book on the *Organization of Programming Languages* gives an overview of the most important topics in the field of programming languages. After some introductory remarks on programming languages we consider syntax and semantics, as well as some compiler aspects, before we start to talk about specific features of programming languages, i.e. data types, expressions and control structures, procedures, data encapsulation, inheritance and concurrency.

1.1   Evolution of Programming Languages

The famous programming language *Tower of Babel* (due to Communications of the ACM, see [SAMM 69], for example) represents the explosion of languages and various dialects of them in the early stages of computer programming languages. Since that time the number of newly introduced programming languages rose once more, but there are still only a few languages which are used by a wider community of programmers. The most important dependencies between languages are shown in Figure 1.1. But let's start at the beginning.

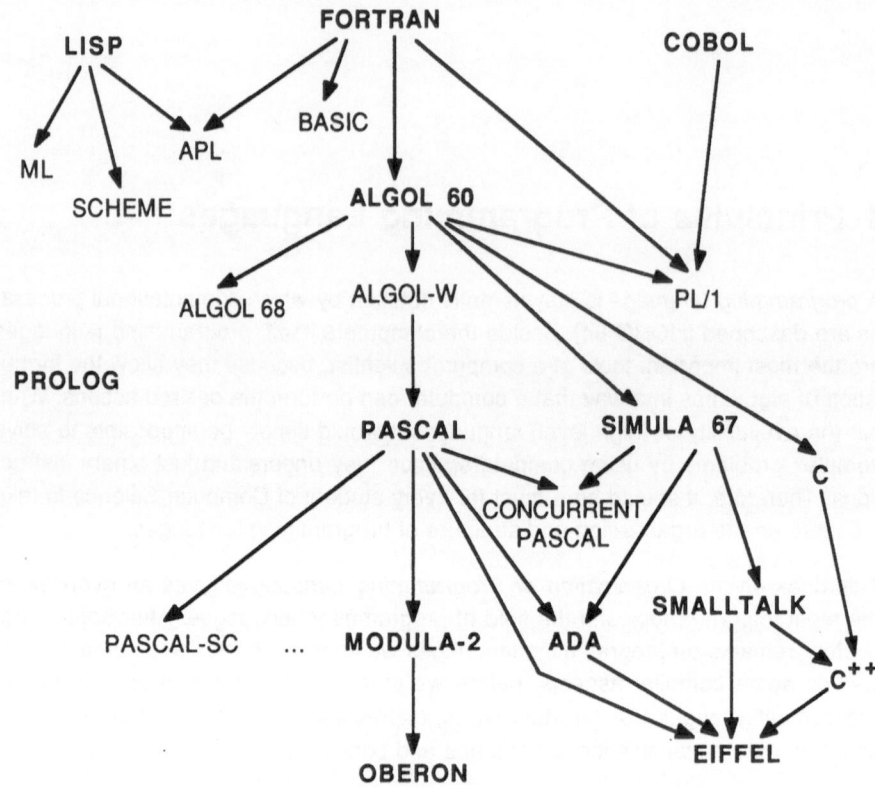

Fig. 1.1. Important language dependencies

First Generation Languages

Computers usually operate on a binary level, i.e. computers understand just sequences of 0's and 1's. Thus, in the early days of computer programming *binary
machine code* was used to program computers. We call such codes first generation
languages, even though there are not less people refusing the term languages for
binary machine code (Sammet, for example, even does not consider assembly
languages to be programming languages, cf [SAMM 69]).

Binary programming means that the program directly reflects the hardware structure of the computer. Sequences of 0's and 1's cause certain actions in processing,
control, or memory units, i.e. programming was done on the flip-flop level. It was
recognized very rapidly that programming computers on binary machine code level
is very troublesome. For example, the insertion of a new instruction - a normal
situation in program development - results in incorrect addresses in the already

existing instructions. Thus, it is obvious that binary programming could not success-
fully be applied to solve complex problems. A small step forward was done by the
introduction of programming in octal or hexadecimal code which caused also the
development of the first "compilation systems." Obviously, this was not enough.

Second Generation Languages

The obvious drawbacks of binary programming became smaller by the introduction
of second generation languages: *assembly languages*. These languages allowed
mnemonic abbreviations as symbolic names and the concept of commands and
operands was introduced. A programmer's work became much easier, since the
symbolic notation and addressing of instructions and data was now possible.
Compilation systems, called *assemblers*, were developed to translate the symbolic
programs into machine code.

Assembly languages still reflect the hardware structure of the target machine - not
on the flip-flop level, but on the register level, i.e. the abstraction has changed from
the flip-flop to the register level. The instruction set of the target computer directly
determines the scope of an assembly language.

With the introduction of linking mechanisms, assembling of code separately became possible and the first steps towards program structuring were recognizable,
although the term structured programming cannot be used for programming
assembly code. The major disadvantage of assembly languages is that programs
are still machine dependent and, in general, only readable by the authors.

Third Generation Languages

Assembly languages were replaced by third generation languages or so-called
high level languages. These languages allow control structures which are based
on logical data objects: variables of a specific type. They provide a level of abstraction allowing machine-independent specification of data, functions or processes,
and their control. A programmer can now focus on the problem to be solved without
being concerned with the internal hardware structure of the target computer.

When considering high level programming languages, there are four groups of
programming languages (and, therefore, programming styles) distinguishable:

- *imperative* programming languages,

- *functional* programming languages,

- *logic* programming languages, and

- *object-oriented* programming languages.

Imperative languages (sometimes also called *procedural languages*) are mostly influenced by the *von Neumann* computer architecture. Typical elements of such languages are *assignment statements*, data structures and type binding, as well as control mechanisms; active procedures manipulate passive data objects. Typical representatives are FORTRAN or PASCAL.

While the assignment statement is central for imperative programming languages, (pure) functional programming languages (sometimes also called *applicative languages*) have no assignment statements. Their syntax is closely related to the formulation of mathematical functions. Thus, *functions* are central for functional programming languages. Typical representatives are LISP or APL.

Logic programming languages (sometimes also called *declarative* or *rule-based languages*) are another group of languages which are totally different from imperative languages (and even from functional languages). *Facts* and *rules* (the logic) are used to represent information (or knowledge) and a logical *inference process* is used to produce results. In contrast to this, control structures are not explicitly defined in a program, they are part of the programming language (inference mechanism). The most important representative is PROLOG.

Object-oriented programming languages form the fourth group of languages supporting a different concept of programming. While in imperative programming languages data and their manipulating procedures form separate units, object-oriented programming languages just know the *object* representing data as well as procedures. Data structures and their appropriate manipulation processes are packed together to form a syntactical unit. Typical representatives are SIMULA 67, SMALLTALK, C++, or EIFFEL.

Often programming languages cannot be clearly associated with one of these four groups. For example, languages like MODULA-2 or OBERON are sometimes said to be imperative although they contain object-oriented features. In the following a brief description of the historical highlights is given.

In the 1950s and early 1960s fundamental concepts on compilers have been developed and the first compilers have been introduced (for example the first FORTRAN compiler, cf [BACK 57]), a precondition for the design of high level programming languages. Now, the first step was done to produce more reliable programs, since structured programming became possible, and to get portability on source code level.

The most important representatives of high level programming languages designed in the 1950s and 1960s are

- FORTRAN,

- ALGOL 60, and

- COBOL.

FORTRAN (*FOR*mula *TRAN*slation) [FORT 66], [TORB 91] and ALGOL 60 (*ALGO*rithmic *Language*) [NAUR 63] were designed to solve numerical scientific problems while COBOL (*CO*mmon *Business Oriented Language*) was introduced to solve business data processing problems. With FORTRAN (developed at IBM by a small group headed by Backus) the ideas of *separate compilation* were introduced, ALGOL 60 introduced *block structures* and *recursive procedures*, while COBOL introduced *data descriptions* and English, i.e. *natural language like program descriptions* (e.g. SUBTRACT TAX FROM PAY is a typical "natural language" like COBOL statement). FORTRAN and COBOL became standards in scientific and commercial programming and are still popular programming languages, not least because of IBM's promotion [FORT 78], [METC 87], [COBO 74]. For them probably come true what once was said about the famous Volkswagen Beetle in a German commercial: "*Er läuft und läuft und läuft und läuft ....*" Not so ALGOL 60. But the influence of ALGOL 60 on other programming languages was much greater, we still talk about *ALGOL-like* languages. At Stanford University Wirth developed ALGOL-W [WIRT 66a] (a language which lies between ALGOL 60 and ALGOL 68) and EULER [WIRT 66b] ("*a trip with the bush knife through the jungle of language features and facilities,*" [WIRT 85]) on the bases of ALGOL 60, and later the probably most successful and most common high level programming language: PASCAL. But ALGOL 60 was also a direct predecessor of PL/1, ALGOL 68, SIMULA 67 and BCPL and, thus, influenced indirectly languages like MODULA-2, C, OBERON, CONCURRENT PASCAL, ADA, SMALLTALK, or EIFFEL.

Beside the development of such conventional programming languages in the '60s there have been serious attempts to define conceptually different languages: LISP, APL, and SNOBOL, for instance. Already in the late 1950s John McCarthy at MIT begun within one of the first artificial intelligence projects to design a recursive system for list processing. The result was LISP (*LIS*t *Processing*) [MCCA 60], [MCCA 65], [JONE 90] a relatively simple language for symbolic expression handling. Among the new features introduced by LISP were *prefix operator notation, recursion, garbage collection* and the basic *concepts of functional programming.* LISP was the first language defined formally in its own language. APL (*A Programming Language*) is also a functional programming language which originally was designed by Iverson at IBM in the early 1960s. In the beginning the language was only defined in a book [IVER 62], i.e. not implemented. The language contains many concepts from mathematics and the original APL was used for a complete formal description of the IBM/360 computer family. SNOBOL (*Stri*N*g Oriented sym*B*Olic Language*) and later SNOBOL4 developed by Farber, Griswold, and Polonsky in the mid 1960s [FARB 64], [GRIS 71] is another language which was not developed in the ALGOL 60 context. SNOBOL was mainly designed for string processing. Thus, its emphasis is on character string data and the appropriate pattern matching features.

Back to imperative programming languages. In the mid 1960s IBM launched a very aspiring project: PL/1 (but its first standard definition report was published more than 10 years later PL/1 76]). This new language PL/1 (*Programming Language 1*) was thought to become a general purpose programming language containing elements from ALGOL 60, FORTRAN, COBOL, and LISP. *Exception handling* and *multi-tasking* were the new features introduced by PL/1. The language was the most complex language of its days and its success is questionable - similar to those other complex languages like ALGOL 68 and ADA. Dijkstra once said about PL/1 in his ACM Turing Award Lecture [DIJK 72]: "*Using PL/1 must be like flying a plane with 7000 buttons, switches, and handles to manipulate in the cockpit.*"

Apropos ALGOL 68. This language is a result of some further developments of ALGOL 60 which were initiated by the IFIP Working Group 2.1. ALGOL 68 introduced the concept of *orthogonality*, i.e. the language consists of a number of elementary constructs which can be arbitrarily composed without causing interactions or unpredictable effects. The ALGOL 68 language report [VANW 69] gives a complete formal specification of the language, which is rather complex. The complexity of the language is as well the reason why a small group of the members of the IFIP WG 2.1 - Hoare and Wirth were among them - were against the publication of this report, without success, as we know. Hoare's and Wirth's interest could already be recognized: The elegance and simplicity of programming languages.

SIMULA 67 was another important language which was designed during the 1960s. Nygaard and Dahl designed SIMULA 1 in the early 1960s at the Norwegian Computing Center and thereafter made further developments which resulted in SIMULA 67 [DAHL 66]. SIMULA was not just another kind of a general purpose language like PL/1, rather it was designed to handle simulation problems. The language is in many of its constructs a direct successor of ALGOL 60. The new feature which was introduced by SIMULA 67 was the *class* concept: a mechanism to group together data structures and procedures to manipulate the data structures. This concept can be seen as the introduction of *abstract data types*. Hierarchies of classes can be defined, and the inheritance concept is applied. The definition of a class is distinct from its instance, i.e. a program can dynamically generate several instances of the same class.

BASIC (*Beginner's All-purpose Symbolic Instruction Code*) is a language which was also designed in the 1960s. It was invented as an educational tool and allows only simple control and data structures. No new features were introduced by BASIC. However, its simplicity is probably the reason for its relatively wide use on personal computers until the end of the 1970s, when BASIC was more and more displaced by PASCAL.

The next decade, the 1970s, started with the introduction of PASCAL [WIRT 71a], [JENS 74]. Although Wirth (now back in Switzerland and a member of the former Fachgruppe Computer-Wissenschaften at the Eidgenössische Technische Hochschule, Zürich) primarily designed PASCAL as a language for teaching, its practical usability was also a design goal: "*In fact, I do not believe in using tools and formalisms in teaching that are inadequate for any practical task*", [WIRT 85]. With PASCAL an elegant programming language was designed from which an efficient code can be generated. PASCAL is mainly based on the ideas of ALGOL 60, but it contains also elements from ALGOL-W (while and case statement) and ALGOL 68 (user defined data types). The language supports strongly the efforts on structural programming and is very attractive because of its possibilities to structure data, especially the possibility of user defined data types. PASCAL gained in significance in the late 1970s, when more and more personal computers and microcomputers came in use.

It took not a long time that Wirth started to work on new ideas: To work out rules for multiprogramming and to find mechanisms to support modularity in program systems. The result was MODULA and later MODULA-2, introduced in the late 1970s [WIRT 78], [WIRT 88a]. MODULA-2 includes all aspects of PASCAL and extends them with the important module concept. Thus, *modules* are the major issues of MODULA-2: program units that can include type definitions, objects, and procedures which can be accessed by other program units. But the sequence of languages that were designed by Niklaus Wirth does not end with MODULA-2. The latest outcome from his research work is called OBERON [WIRT88b], [WIRT 88c], [WIRT 90]. OBERON is based on MODULA-2, it has a few additions (e.g. the facility of extended record types) and several subtractions (e.g. local moduls were eliminated in OBERON, since the experience with MODULA-2 has shown that they are rarely used, [WIRT 88b]). Wirth's motto for the design of OBERON was Einstein's word: "*Make it as simple as possible, but not simpler*" [WIRT 88c].

Back to the 1970s. There was an imperative language, a logical language, and an object-oriented language introduced which have to be mentioned here: C, PRO-LOG, and SMALLTALK. C [KERN 78], [KERN 88] is a successor of CPL (*Combined Programming Language*), and BCPL (*Basic CPL*), [RICH 69]. Kernighan and Ritchie introduce C in their report in the following way, [KERN 88]: "*C is a general purpose programming language which features economy of expression, modern control flow and data structures, and a rich set of operators. C is not a 'very high level' language, nor a 'big' one, and is not specialized to any particular area of application.*" Since C was originally designed for the implementation of the UNIX operating system, it is closely related with UNIX and makes programming in a UNIX environment easy. Although there were (and still are) considerable critical voices about C, the popularity of C grew with the popularity of UNIX.

PROLOG (*PRO*gramming in *LOG*ic) was designed by Roussel and Colmerauer of Groupe Intelligence Artificielle at the University of Marseille in cooperation with Kowalski of the Department of Artificial Intelligence at the University of Edinburgh in the early 1970s. This logic programming language has become *that* language in the field of artificial intelligence not least because the Japanese government announced in 1981 the Fifth Generation Computer Systems (FGCS) project to be based on PROLOG. Knowledge bases are build in PROLOG by specifying facts and rules, then queries are evaluated on this symbolic logic. PROLOG makes use of formalisms and inference mechanisms of mathematical logic [CLOC 81], [GIAN 86], [STER 90].

SMALLTALK is a result of the ideas which Alan Kay at the University of Utah had already in the late '60s. He saw the potential of personal computers and the necessity of a programming environment for non-programmers. In the early 1970s Kay designed at Xerox PARC the language FLEX, which is a predecessor of SMALLTALK. Data and procedures manipulating the data are objects, and SMALLTALK is probably the most prominent representative of object-oriented languages. The communication between objects is done by *messages*. Objects can return other objects in reply to a message [GOLD 83].

But there is one more language which cannot be forgotten when talking about the evolution of programming languages: ADA [ADA 79], [BYNE 91]. The design of ADA was a very ambitious and expensive project launched by the US Department of Defense (DoD). ADA was thought to become a general purpose language for large software projects providing all the state-of-the-art concepts of conventional programming languages and, therefore, being an instrument against what is called software crisis. The major concepts of ADA are: Modularity, data abstraction, separate compilation, exception handling, concurrency, and generic procedures. There exist very controversial opinions about ADA and its usability. The most critical points of ADA are its *size* and *complexity*. ADA's objectives were *readability* and *simplicity* to make reliable programs possible and maintenance easy. But exactly these objectives were *not achieved* by the design of ADA, what rises the question, whether ADA programs are reliable and secure. Hoare, one of the advisers of the project, is therefore very critical about the usage of ADA and he appealed to the representatives of the programming profession in the US and to all concerned with the welfare and safety of mankind [HOAR 81]: "*Do not allow this language in its present state to be used in applications where reliability is critical, i.e. nuclear power stations, cruise missiles, early warning systems ... An unreliable programming language generating unreliable programs constitutes a far greater risk to our environment and to our society than unsafe cars, toxic pesticides, or accidents at nuclear power stations. Be vigilant to reduce that risk, not to increase it.*" Here, the sense of responsibility of all computer scientists is required.

In the last four decades much more languages and dialects of these languages have been designed. Lets consider PASCAL, for example, there exist several specialized extensions: CONCURRENT PASCAL [BRIN 75a], UCSD PASCAL [BOWL 79], PASCAL PLUS [BUST 78], PASCAL/R [SCHM 80], or PASCAL-SC [BOHL 81], to name only a few of these extensions, subsets, or dialects. But its beyond the scope of this text to give a complete historical overview of programming languages. The selection was based on the importance of the languages.

Fourth Generation Languages

Fourth generation languages deal with the following two fields which become more and more important:

- database and query languages, and

- program or application generators.

The steadily increasing usage of software packages like database systems, spread sheets, statistical packages, and other (special purpose) packages makes it necessary to have a medium of control available which can easily be used by non-specialists. In fourth generation languages the user describes *what* he wants to be solved, instead of *how* he wants to solve a problem - as it is done using procedural languages. In general, fourth generation languages are not only languages, but interactive programming environments.

One of the best known database query languages is probably SQL (*Structured Query Language*): a query language for relational databases which was developed at IBM and which is based on Codd's requirements for non-procedural query languages for relational databases. NATURAL is another approach in this field emphazising on a structured programming style. Program or application generators are often based on a certain specification method and produce an output (e.g. a high level program) to an appropriate specification. There exist already a great number of fourth generation languages:

- ADF,

- IDEAL,

- NATURAL,

- NOMAD,

- MANTIS,

- MAPPER, or

- RAMIS

to name only a few. An overview of such languages is given in [MART 86]. A performance analysis of several fourth generation languages and their comparison with third generation COBOL programs is given in [MATO 89].

1.2   Backus, Hoare, and Wirth

In this Section we want to give a brief overview of the views of *Backus*, *Hoare*, and *Wirth*, three Computer Scientists whose work is closely related with the definition, design, and development of programming languages. All of them are recipients of the *ACM Turing Award*.

John Backus received the Award in 1977 for his "*profound, influential, and lasting contributions to the design of practical high-level programming systems, notably through his work on FORTRAN, and for seminal publication of formal procedures for the specification of programming languages* [ACM 78]."

Charles Antony Richard Hoare received the Award in 1980 for his "*fundamental contributions to the definition and design of programming languages. ... He is best known for his work on axiomatic definitions of programming languages through the use of techniques popularly referred to as axiomatic semantics. He ... was responsible for inventing and promulgating advanced data structuring techniques in scientific programming languages* [ACM 81]."

Niklaus Wirth was presented the 1984 Turing Award "*in recognition of his outstanding work in developing a sequence of innovative computer languages: EULER, ALGOL-W, MODULA, and PASCAL. ... The hallmarks of a Wirth language are its simplicity, economy of design, and high-quality engineering, which result in a language whose notation appears to be a natural extension of algorithmic thinking rather than an extraneous formalism* [ACM 85]."

In the following we quote from their Turing Award Lectures [BACK 78], [HOAR 81], and [WIRT 85].

John Backus

John Backus describes basic defects in the framework of conventional languages and suggests them to be responsible for the expressive weakness and cancerous growth of such languages. He suggests applicative or functional languages as an alternative:

Conventional programming languages are large, complex, and inflexible. Their limited expressive power is inadequate to justify their size and cost. In order to understand the problems of conventional programming languages, their intellectual parent - the von Neumann computer - must be examined. Von Neumann computers are build around a bottle-neck: the word-at-a-time tube connecting the CPU and the store. Conventional languages are basically high level, complex versions of the von Neumann computer. Thus variable = storage cells; assignment statements = fetching, storing, and arithmetic; control statements = jump and test instructions. The symbol ":=" is the linguistic von Neumann bottle-neck. Von Neumann languages split programming into a world of expressions and a world of statements; the first of these is an orderly world, the second is a disorderly one, a world that structured programming has simplified somewhat, but without attacking the basic problems of the split itself and of the word-at-a-time style of conventional languages.

When comparing a von Neumann program and a functional program for inner product, a number of problems of the former and advantages of the latter can be illustrated: e.g., the von Neumann program is repetitive and word-at-a-time, works only for two vectors with given names and length, and can only be made general by use of a procedure declaration, which has complex semantics. The functional program is non-repetitive, deals with vectors as units, is more hierarchically constructed, is completely general, and creates "housekeeping" operations by composing high-level housekeeping operators. It does not name its arguments, hence it requires no procedure declaration. The defects of conventional languages cannot be resolved unless a new kind of language framework is discovered.

Backus studied the area of non-von Neumann systems very carefully and his search indicates a useful approach to designing non-von Neumann languages. This approach involves four elements:

- A functional style of programming without variables.

- An algebra of functional programs.

- A formal functional programming system.

- Applicative state transition systems.

Charles Antony Richard Hoare

In the early 1960s, when designing a modest subset of ALGOL 60 for the implementation on the then next computer generation, Hoare adopted certain basic principles which he believes to be as valid today as they were then:

i) Security. The principle that every syntactically incorrect program should be rejected by the compiler and that every syntactically correct program should give a result or an error message that is predictable and comprehensible in terms of the source language program itself.

ii) Brevity of the object code produced by the compiler and compactness of run time working data. There is a clear reason for this: The size of main storage on any computer is limited and its extension involves delay and expense.

iii) Entry and exit conventions for procedures and functions should be as compact and efficient as for tightly coded machine code subroutines. Since procedures are one of the most powerful features of high level languages, there must be no impediment to their frequent use.

iv) The compiler should use only a single pass. It has to be structured as a collection of mutually recursive procedures, each capable of analyzing and translating a major syntactic unit of the language.

Hoare advocates these principles also when being a member of the ALGOL committee or when being an adviser to the DoD ADA project. But in both cases his advices died away unheard. His warnings and suggestions:

- When any new language design project is nearing completion, there is always a mad rush to get new features added before standardization. The rush is mad indeed, because it leads into a trap from which there is no escape. A feature which is omitted can always be added later, when its design and its implications are well understood. A feature which is included before it is fully understood can never be removed later.

- Programming is complex because of the large number of conflicting objectives for each of our programming projects. If our basic tool, the language in which we design and code our programs, is also complicated, the language itself becomes part of the problem rather than part of its solution.

- It would be impossible to write a wholly reliable compiler for a language of this complexity (PL/1) and impossible to write a wholly reliable program when the correctness of each part of the program depends on checking that every other part of the program has avoided all the traps and pitfalls of the language.

- The price of reliability is the pursuit of the utmost simplicity.

- If you want a language with no subsets, you must make it small.

Niklaus Wirth

Nicklaus Wirth recognizes that the complex world around us often requires complex mechanisms. However, this should not diminish our desire for elegant solutions, which convince by their clarity and effectiveness. Simple, elegant solutions are more effective, but they are harder to find than complex ones. His principal aim was and still is simplicity and modularity in program systems.

Evidently, programs should be designed according to the same principles as electronic circuits, that is, clearly subdivided into parts with only a few wires going across the bounderies. Only by understanding one part at a time there would be hope of finally understanding the whole. This attempt received a vigorous starting impulse from the appearance of the report on ALGOL 60. ALGOL 60 was the first language defined with clarity; its syntax was even specified in a rigourous formalism. The lesson was that a clear specification is a necessary but not sufficient condition for a reliable and effective implementation.

The size of the ALGOL-W compiler grew beyond the limits within which one could rest comfortably with the feeling of having a grasp, a mental understanding, of the whole program. Systems programming requires an efficient compiler generating efficient code that operated without a fixed, hidden, and large so-called run-time package. This goal had been missed by both ALGOL-W and PL/1, both because the languages were complex and the target computers inadequate. Wirth overcame these drawbacks with PASCAL and most of all with the combination of MODULA-2 and the Lilith-workstation.

The module is the key to bringing under one hat the contradictory requirements of high level abstraction for security through redundancy checking and low level facilities that allow access to individual features of a particular computer. It lets the programmer encapsulated the use of low level facilities in a few small parts of the system, thus protecting him from falling into their traps in unexpected places.

Wirth distilled a few characteristics which were common to all of his projects:

- The bootstrap principle. Bootstrapping is the most effective way of profiting from one's own efforts as well as suffering from one's mistakes.

- An early distinction between what is essential and what ephemeral. Rejecting pressures to include all kinds of facilities that "might also be nice to have" is sometimes hard. The danger that one's desire to please will interfere with the goal of consistent design is very real. One has to weigh the gains against the cost. But even if the effort of building unnecessarily large systems and the cost of memory to contain their code could be ignored, the real cost is hidden in the unseen efforts of the innumerable programmers trying desperately to understand them and use them effectively.

- The choice of tools. A tool should be commensurate with the project; it must be as simple as possible, but not simpler. A tool is in fact counterproductive when a large part of the entire project is taken up by mastering the tool.

- Every single project was primarily a learning project. One learns best when inventing, and teaching by setting a good example is often the most effective method and sometimes the only one available.

Rèsumè

While Backus sees the cause of most problems of todays programming systems in the von Neumann bottle-neck and the great influence of the von Neumann computer architecture to the design of programming languages, both Hoare and Wirth see the evil in the cruse of complexity. Backus suggests a functional style of programming and, thus, functional programming languages influencing the hardware design of new computers (and not vice versa).

Hoare and Wirth are advocates of simplicity and modularity, since simple and elegant solutions are prerequisites for reliable - and therefore successful - systems. The disaster with all these well-known highly complex programming languages proofs their views. We think that just changing from imperative to functional, logical, or object-oriented languages and programming styles does not help much; we have also to consider the principle of simplicity - no matter what kind of language we use.

1.3   The Concept of Abstraction

The most important concept introduced by high level languages is *abstraction*, which is a process that allows the general pattern to be observed while ignoring the inessential details (cf Figure 1.2). Thus, we mean the process of crystallizing the essentials for a problem's solution, i.e. this knowledge about the real world, which is relevant to get the desired results. Implementation details and certain irrelevant properties will be hidden for clarity. An abstraction is thereby also a simplification of facts [WIRT 76].

An example of abstraction could be the description of a memory cell as a location to store data values, the physical details are of no interest from a programmer's point of view. Abstraction has a twofold relationship with programming languages [GHEZ 82]:

- Programming languages are used to implement abstract models.

- Programming languages are hardware abstractions.

Along with the evolution of programming languages we can recognize an evolution of the latter relationship. While binary or octal code was just a low level abstraction of the flip-flop hardware level, with the introduction of assembler code we find the abstraction on the register level, and finally with higher level languages the abstraction is based on logical data objects (variables) and their control. Thus, two principle mechanisms of abstraction can be distinguished:

• Data abstraction.

• Control abstraction.

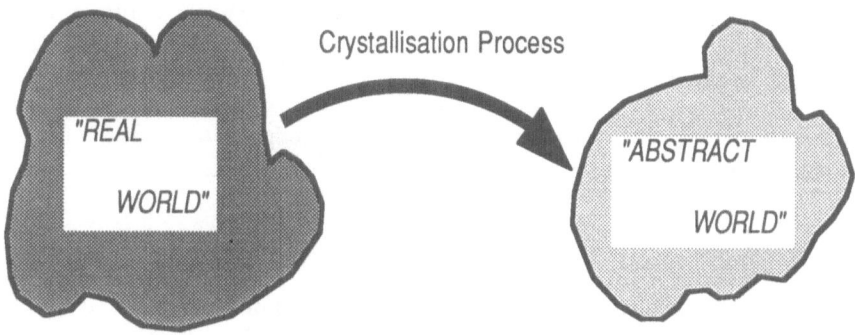

Fig. 1.2. Concept of Abstraction

Data abstraction is a mechanism providing types and allowing the declaration of variables of these types, as well as providing operations for the manipulation of these variables. Thus, data abstraction in its simplest form is given by standard types such as *real*, for example. In high level programming languages the data type *real* allows the definition of floating-point variables, and the set of operations on this data type allow the arithmetic manipulation of objects of this type.

The next step in data abstraction is given by the possibility of user-defined data types. But this is only one half of the abstraction, since the manipulation of variables of those user-defined data types is not clearly given in form of operations which can be applied to those data types. Afford reliefs the introduction of *abstract data types*:

• An abstract data type is a (user-defined) data type and the set of permitted operations on objects of this type, by which the internal representation is hidden to those using that type.

Control abstraction is the mechanism defining the order in which certain activities or groups of activities should be performed. By this we mean not only control structures on the statement level like conditional and unconditional branching, but also the construction of subprograms up to concurrent programs. Control abstraction on the subprogram level was already introduced in assembler languages by allowing macro definitions.

1.4   Basic Terminology and Language Descriptions

Defining a programming language means describing the syntax and semantic of that language. We will have a closer look at these two aspects of (programming) languages in the beginning of Chapter 2. The objective of this section is to introduce the basic terminology of formal languages and to give an introduction to formal methods for the *description of the syntax*, i.e. the syntactical form of a programming language. Two formalisms are of special interest: *Backus-Naur form* (BNF) and *syntax diagrams*.

But before starting with meta-languages for the description of programming languages, we should define some of the most important elements of languages.

Definitions

- *Alphabet*: An alphabet is an arbitrary but finite set of *symbols*. For example, machine code is based on the binary alphabet $A_1 = \{0, 1\}$; other examples are $A_2 = \{0, 1, 2, 3, 4, 5, 6, 7, 8, 9\}$, $A_3 = \{+, -, *, /\}$ etc.

- *Symbols*: The elements of the vocabulary (alphabet) of a formal language are called symbols, while for natural languages we call them *words*.

- *Token*: Multiple occurrences of symbols (or words) are called tokens.

- *Sentence*: A sequence of symbols is called a sentence.

- *Grammar (Syntax)*: The grammar or the syntax of a language defines the form of the language, this means whether an arbitrary sequence of symbols is correct. We will say that a correct sentence will be accepted by the language.

- *Semantics*: The meaning of correct sentences of a language is defined by semantic rules. In general, we have no formal description of the semantics of a language.

- *String*: A (finite) sequence of elements of a certain set (alphabet) is called a string. In analogy to the empty set in set theory we can consider an

empty string ε. The *empty string ε* is that string which contains no symbols. The sequence 0011 is an example of a string over the alphabet A_1.

- *Production*: Rules for string substitution are called productions. The symbols → and ::= are widely used to represent productions. For example,
  the rule (production)

  $$s \rightarrow a\ b \qquad (or\ s ::= a\ b\ )$$

  means that s can be substituted by a b, or s is defined as a b.

- *Terminal symbols*: The symbols which actually occur in a sentence are
  called terminal symbols. They will never occur on the left side of a production. The symbols **begin**, **end**, **if**, **then**, **else** are an example for
  terminal symbols belonging to the grammar which describes PASCAL.
  Terminal symbols must be valid symbols of the language. T indicates the
  set of terminal symbols, while T^* indicates the set of all possible strings
  over T.

- *Nonterminal symbols*: The nonterminal symbols must be defined by
  other productions, i.e. they occur also on the left side of productions.
  Nonterminal symbols are syntactical variables. N indicates the set of
  nonterminal symbols, while N^* indicates the set of all possible strings
  over N.

- *Vocabulary = Alphabet*: Like natural languages, formal languages are
  based on a specific vocabulary, i.e. the elements of the language. The
  vocabulary of a formal language is the union of the terminal and nonterminal symbols. $V = N \cup T$ indicates the vocabulary, while V^* indicates the
  set of all possible strings over V.

The * in these definitions indicates the *closure* of a certain set. We will find a similar
usage of this operator for productions.

BNF

Backus-Naur form (BNF) was first introduced for the definition of the syntactical
structure of the programming language ALGOL 60 (cf. [NAUR 63]). It is the most
popular form for the precise syntactical definition of programming languages.

The Backus-Naur form is a so-called *meta-language*, i.e. a language which is used
to describe other languages. A BNF rule or production defines a (single) nonterminal symbol by other nonterminals and/or terminal symbols using the "→" as the
defining symbol (cf Table 1.1). On the left side of an arrow only nonterminals can
occur, while on the right side both terminals and nonterminals are allowed. There
exist a lot of dialects of the BNF-notation. Table 1.1 shows some common (meta-)
symbols of the BNF.

Table 1.1.   BNF-notation

symbol	meaning
→	"is defined as"
.	end of a definition
		"or", alternative
[x]	one or no occurrence of x
{ x }	an arbitrary occurrence of x (0, 1, 2, ...)
(x | y)	selection (x or y)

Using this notation and the set of terminal symbols

> T   =   { +, -, 0, 1, 2, 3, 4, 5, 6, 7, 8, 9 } ,

as well as the set of nonterminal symbols

> N   =   { int, unsigned_int, digit } ,

we can define integers by the following BNF-rules (productions):

> int   →   [+ | -] unsigned_int .
> unsigned_int   →   digit | unsigned_int digit .
> digit   →   0 | 1 | 2 | 3 | 4 | 5 | 6 | 7 | 8 | 9 .

The first rule defines that an integer is an unsigned integer with a leading sign. This sign can be absent, or "+", or "-". The second rule shows that BNF allows recursive definitions.

A formal description of a language is given, if a finite number of BNF-rules exists, allowing the derivation of any sentence of the language. In this sense, the finite set of rules given above is a formal description of the infinite set of integers. A sentence is correct if there exists a set of BNF-productions which allows the derivation of that sentence. Obviously, the Backus-Naur form (as well as the below introduced syntax diagrams) are preferably used in the syntax analysis phase of compilers.

Syntax Diagrams

One way to represent the syntactical structure of a language is to use the BNF-notation. *Syntax diagrams* or *graphs* are another - a graphical - way to represent the syntax of a language. The graphical syntax representation makes a language definition easy to survey.

The language representation with syntax graphs is equivalent to the representation using BNF. According to [WIRT 81] we introduce six rules that allow the transformation of a BNF-notation into a syntax graph.

R1.   Productions of the form

$$N \quad \rightarrow \quad \alpha_1 \mid \alpha_2 \mid \ldots \mid \alpha_n$$

will be represented by the following graph:

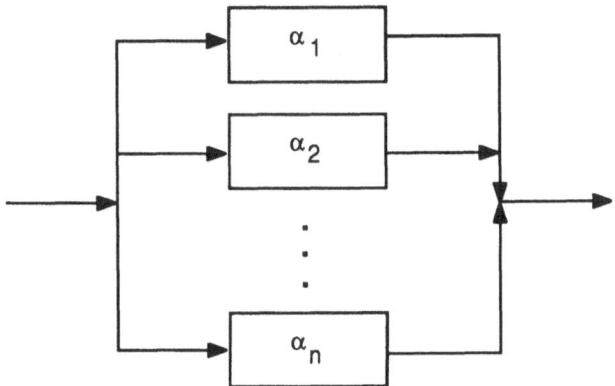

R2.   Terms of the form

$$\alpha \quad = \quad a_1 \; a_2 \; \ldots \; a_n$$

will be represented by the following graph:

R3.   If an element has one or no occurrence, i.e.

$$[\alpha] \, ,$$

it will be represented by the following graph:

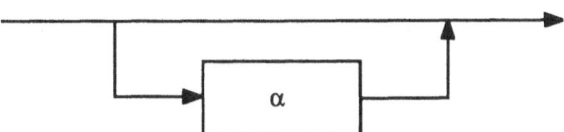

R4.   If an element is arbitrarily repeated (inclusive 0 times), i.e.

$$\{\alpha\} \, ,$$

it will be represented by the following graph:

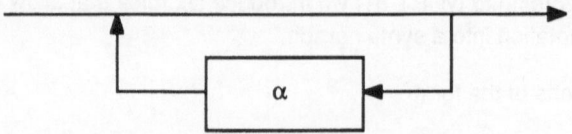

R5. Nonterminal symbols N will be represented within a rectangle:

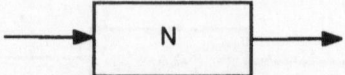

R6. Terminal symbols t will be represented within a circle or an oval:

Obviously, a given sentence will be correct, if and only if the elements of the sentence describe a correct path through the graphs. Using the rules R1 - R6 we can transform the BNF-notation for integers as given above into the following syntax graphs.

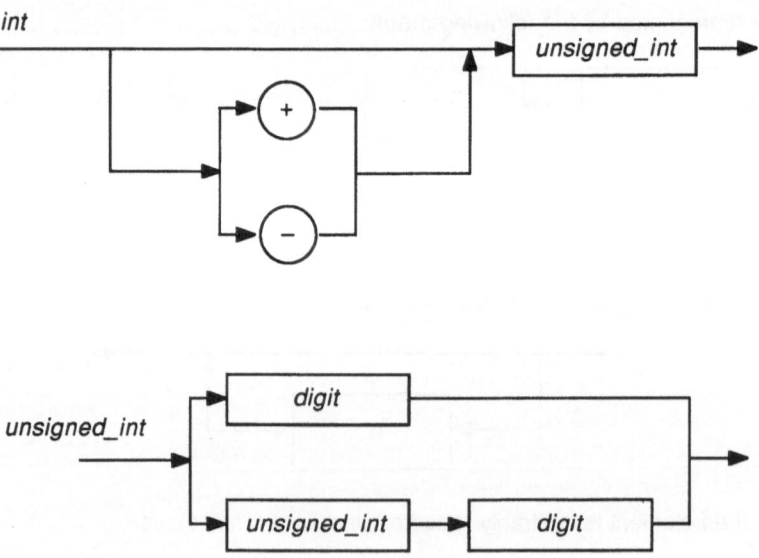

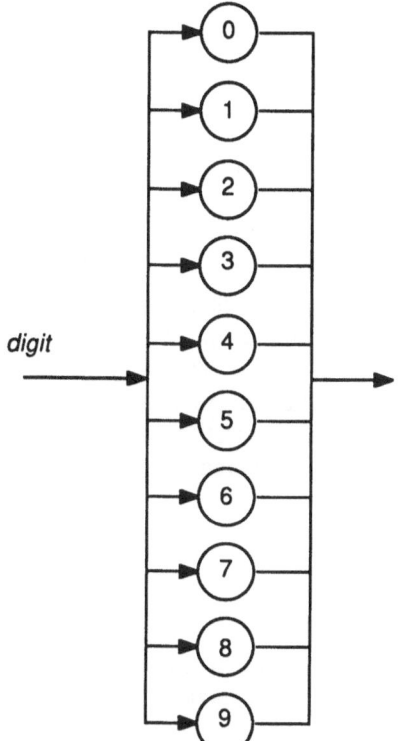

2 Language Processing

Each language − no matter whether it is a natural or a programming language − has a *syntax* and a *semantic*. These two language aspects are considered and compared in Chapter 2.1. It is followed by a brief introduction to formal languages and grammars. Since programming languages are only of interest for a wider community if they are implemented (i.e. if there exists a compiler) on a certain computer, we will finally give a brief overview and introduction to the major implementation techniques of programming languages.

2.1 Syntax vs Semantics

The *syntax* of a programming language describes the *form* of the language. It is defined by certain rules. These syntactic rules describe the way in which we have to combine the basic elements (the terminal symbols) of a programming language to generate correct sentences, i.e. sentences which will be accepted by the grammar of the language (see below).

The meaning of such syntactically correct sentences of the language is defined by *semantic rules*. Semantic rules describe the *effect* of correct sentences. Wirth describes very clearly the correlation between syntax and semantics [WIRT 81]: "*Die Syntax dient letztlich immer einem höheren Ziel, nämlich einer Codierung einer bestimmten Bedeutung.*"

For example, by explicitly giving the sentence

```
k   :   integer;
```

we can explain how integer variables are defined in PASCAL. The semantics of this statement tells us that space for an integer variable is reserved which - if the statement is contained in the declaration part of a procedure - can only be accessed during the existence of that block in which it is declared. Then, considering

```
k   :=   k + 1;
```

purely from a syntactical viewpoint, "k", ":=", "+", "1", and ";" are just symbols; "1" has nothing to do with the mathematical object 1. A semantic description of PASCAL (say) might relate "k := k + 1;" to the idea of incrementing the contents of some memory cell.

Another example. The syntax of WHILE-statements, for instance, in OBERON is given in BNF-notation in the following way:

$$WhileStatement \rightarrow \textbf{WHILE}\ expression\ \textbf{DO}\ StatementSequence\ \textbf{END}.$$

The meaning is that the *StatementSequence* is repeatedly executed as long as *expression* is true, and *expression* is evaluated before each execution of *StatementSequence*.

While we already know some good formalisms - Backus-Naur form and syntax diagrams - by which the syntax of nearly all new programming languages is described, as yet there is no equivalent semantic formalism available which achieved the popularity of BNF or syntax diagrams. Thus, the semantics of programming languages are still often described in natural language which usually is not concise enough, as we know. Thus, problems arise not only for programmers using such a language, but most of all for the compiler writer who has to implement the language. Anyhow, we want to introduce some methods for formal description of semantics in Chapter 9.

2.2   Formal Languages and Grammars

In this section we give a brief introduction to formal languages. The field of formal languages is a wide area and an independent field of research. A fundamental introduction to this topic will be beyond the scope of this text. For a more detailed description on the theory of formal languages we therefore refer to the books [KUIC 86], [SALO 73], for example.

Grammars and Languages

A complete syntactical description of a language - using, for example, BNF-rules - is called a *grammar*. A grammar G is defined as a 4-tuple G (T, N, P, S), where

- T is the set of terminal symbols,

- N is the set of nonterminal symbols,

- P is the set of productions,

• S ∈ N is the start symbol.

Thus, a grammar consists of a set of rules, where each nonterminal symbol is defined. One of the nonterminal symbols is marked as a *start symbol* of the grammar. For example, such a start symbol could be "PROGRAM" or "MODULE" when considering the languages PASCAL or MODULA-2, respectively.

A (*formal*) *language* L is characterized with reference to a grammar G:

$$L(G) = L(T, N, P, S).$$

We say that a string β can be *directly derived* from a string α

$$\alpha \rightarrow \beta$$

if there exists just one production to produce β from α, e.g.

$$\alpha = \alpha_1 \alpha_2 \alpha_3$$
$$\beta = \alpha_1 \beta_2 \alpha_3$$

and there exists the production

$$\alpha_2 \rightarrow \beta_2.$$

We say that a string α_n can be *derived* from a string α_0, if and only if there exists a sequence of strings $\alpha_0, \alpha_1, \alpha_2, \dots, \alpha_{n-1}$ so that each α_i can directly be derived by α_{i-1} (i = 1, 2, ..., n):

$$\alpha_0 \rightarrow \alpha_1 \rightarrow \alpha_2 \rightarrow \dots \rightarrow \alpha_{n-1} \rightarrow \alpha_n$$

A sequence of such productions will be abbreviated with $\rightarrow^*$:

$$\alpha_0 \rightarrow^* \alpha_n \equiv (\exists \alpha_i, i = 1, 2, \dots, n : \alpha_{i-1} \rightarrow \alpha_i)$$

and $\rightarrow^*$ is said to be the *reflexive transitive closure* of $\rightarrow$.

Now, we can define a language L (G) as the set of all strings of terminal symbols which can be derived from the start symbol S :

$$L = \{\sigma \mid S \rightarrow^* \sigma \text{ and } \sigma \in T^*\}.$$

Considering the derivation process we can find two important strategies: *leftmost derivations* and *rightmost derivations*. A derivation is called leftmost (rightmost) if always the leftmost (rightmost) nonterminal is replaced.

A BNF-rule

$$v \quad \rightarrow \quad \sigma$$

specifies that a (single) nonterminal symbol $v \in N$ can be replaced by $\sigma \in (N \cup T)^*$ regardless of the context in which v occurs. Such productions will be called *context-free*.

According to N. Chomsky we call a grammar and the corresponding language context-free, if and only if it can be defined with a set of context-free productions. Context-free grammars are very important in the theory of programming languages, since the languages they define are, in general, simple in their structure. Parsing techniques are usually based on context-free grammars.

A context-free grammar will be called *unambiguous*, if and only if there exists just one rightmost (leftmost) derivation and therefore one parse tree for each sentence which can be derived by the productions of the grammar. Otherwise it will be called *ambiguous*.

A sentence of an ambiguous grammar can have more than one parse tree and, therefore, it can have more than one meaning. Thus, ambiguous grammars are not very useful for the analysis and the definition of programming languages. They are hard to handle and we normally try to transform them into unambiguous ones. It should be noted, that it is an undecidable problem to determine whether a given grammar is ambiguous or not. As we will see later, there exist some conditions, which - if fulfilled - are sufficient to say that a certain grammar is unambiguous. But these conditions are not necessary, that means that a grammar which does not fulfil these conditions cannot be said to be ambiguous (or even unambiguous).

Hierarchy of Grammars

Grammars are classified according to their complexity. This classification - often referred to as *Chomsky-Hierarchy* - is given by increasing the restrictions on the form of the productions (cf. Figure 2.1).

Type 0 grammars are *no-restriction grammars*, i.e. there are no restrictions neither for the left side, nor for the right side of the productions. Such general grammars are of no relevance for today's programming languages. Writing a parser for a type 0 grammar would be a very hard task. The form of the productions of type 1 grammars implies that replacements can only be done within a certain context, i.e. these are *context-sensitive grammars*. In contrast to that, type 2 grammars are *context-free grammars*, while the left- and right-linear type 3 grammars are *regular grammars*. Clearly, a grammar of type $i + 1$ is also of type i, $i = 0, 1, 2$.

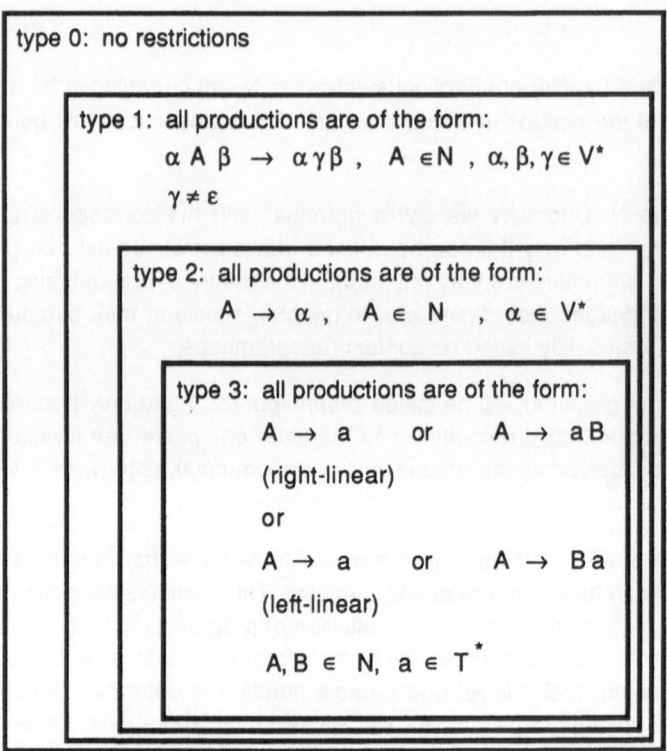

type 0: no restrictions

type 1: all productions are of the form:

$$\alpha\,A\,\beta \;\rightarrow\; \alpha\,\gamma\,\beta\;, \quad A \in N\;,\; \alpha,\beta,\gamma \in V^*$$
$$\gamma \neq \varepsilon$$

type 2: all productions are of the form:

$$A \;\rightarrow\; \alpha\;, \quad A \in N\;,\; \alpha \in V^*$$

type 3: all productions are of the form:

$$A \rightarrow a \qquad \text{or} \qquad A \rightarrow aB$$
(right-linear)

or

$$A \rightarrow a \qquad \text{or} \qquad A \rightarrow Ba$$
(left-linear)

$$A, B \in N,\; a \in T^*$$

Fig. 2.1. Chomsky-Hierarchy

For i = 0, 1, 2, 3, we term a language of type i, if it is generated by a grammar of type i, i.e. a context-free grammar generates a context-free language and a regular grammar generates a regular language, etc. From the compiler writer's view, type 2 and type 3 grammars are the most important ones. While context-free grammars (which, by the way, directly correspond to Backus-Naur forms) define the syntax of declarations, statements, and expressions, etc. (i.e. the structure of a program), the regular grammars define the syntax of identifiers, numbers, strings, etc. (i.e. the basic symbols of the language). Thus, context-free grammars can normally be found in syntactical analysis, while regular grammars are used as a basis of lexical analysis.

Parse Trees

Up to now, we have shown that a grammar can be used to generate sentences of a specific language. However, a compiler has to check strings of symbols to see whether they belong to that language, i.e. to find how a sequence of symbols might be derived from the start symbol using the productions of the grammar and to display the derivation (or to show that the sentence cannot be derived from the start symbol). This problem is known as the *parsing problem*.

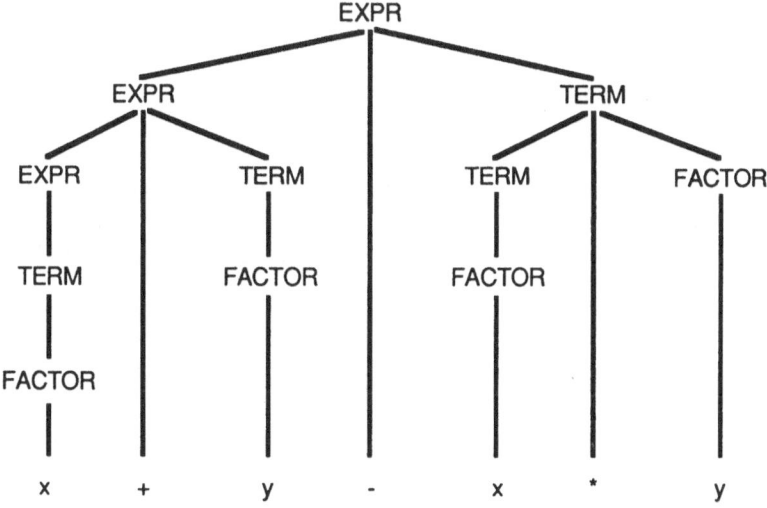

Fig. 2.2. Parse tree for the expression x + y − x * y

The derivation process can be illustrated by a tree as shown in the following. To exemplify this, we define a grammar G_0 (T_0, N_0, P_0, S_0) which accepts arithmetic expressions like x + y − x * y.

$$
\begin{aligned}
T_0 &= &&\{\, x, y, +, -, *, /, (,)\,\} \\
N_0 &= &&\{\, EXPR, TERM, FACTOR\,\} \\
P_0 &= &&\{\, EXPR \;\rightarrow\; TERM \mid EXPR + TERM \mid EXPR - TERM \\
& &&\;\; TERM \;\rightarrow\; FACTOR \mid TERM * FACTOR \mid TERM / FACTOR \\
& &&\;\; FACTOR \rightarrow x \mid y \mid (EXPR)\,\} \\
S_0 &= &&\{\, EXPR\,\}
\end{aligned}
$$

We see that each expression is a sequence of terms which are separated with "+" or "−". Figure 2.2 shows the parse tree for the expression x + y − x * y . It represents graphically the derivation of a sentence of the language according to the grammar G_0 (T_0, N_0, P_0, S_0).

Considering a context-free grammar, we can state the following properties of a parse tree (according to [AHOS 86]):

- The root is marked with the start symbol.

- Each leaf is marked with a terminal symbol or with ε.

- Each node is marked with a nonterminal symbol.

The process of generating a parse tree for a given expression will be called *syntax analysis* or *parsing*.

2.3   Compiler Aspects

Compiling a program means *analysis* and *synthesis* of that program, i.e. determining the structure and meaning of a source code and translating that source code into an equivalent machine code. The major tasks or phases of a compiler are *lexical analysis*, *syntax analysis*, *semantic analysis*, and *code generation*. (cf Fig. 2.3).

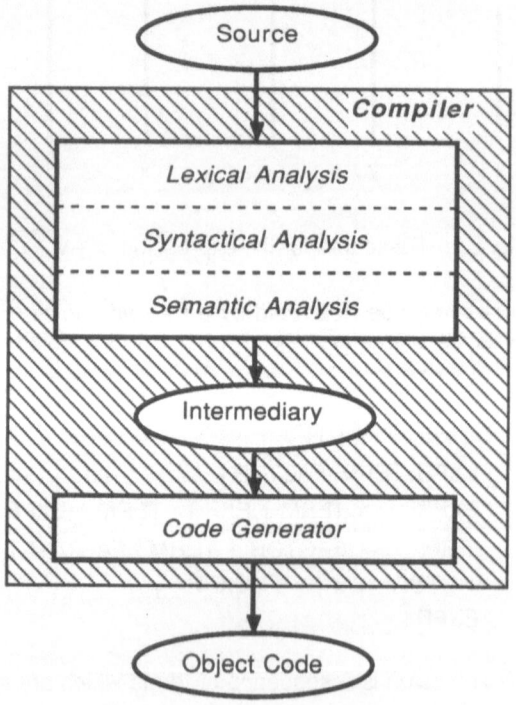

Fig. 2.3.   Compiler phases

Lexical Analysis

At the beginning of the compilation process the source code of a program is nothing else, but a stream of characters. Thus, the task of the *lexical analysis* is to *recognize* symbols (which can be defined by regular grammars) in this stream of characters and to provide these symbols in a more useful representation to the syntax analysis.

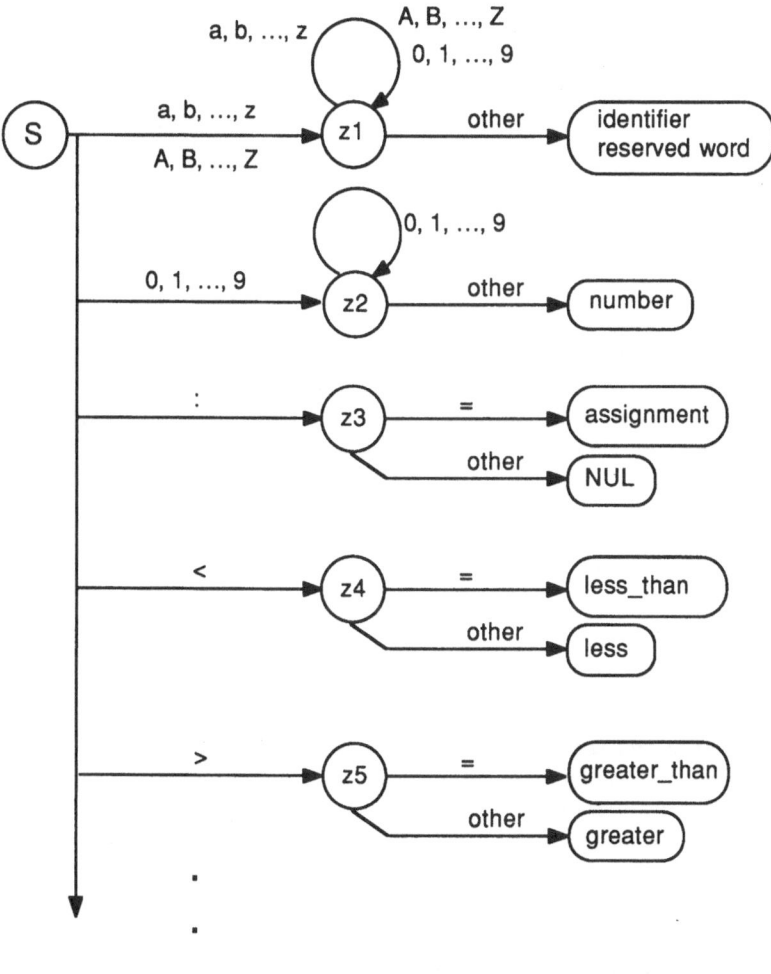

Fig. 2.4. Rudimentary transition diagram for a scanner for an imperative language

The lexical analysis part of a compiler is called *scanner*. Typical functions of a scanner are:

- Skipping spaces, comments, etc.

- Recognizing identifiers and keywords.

- Recognizing constants and numerals.

- Generation of a compiler listing.

The lexical analysis of a program is preferably based on finite deterministic automata, since there is a direct relationship between regular grammars and finite automata, i.e. for each regular grammar it is possible to design a finite automaton which accepts the sentences of the language defined by the grammar. Figure 2.4 shows the transition diagram of an automaton which recognizes the basic elements of an usual imperative programming language. The conversion of such an automaton into a program is not very difficult (cf [TEUF 89], for example).

Syntax Analysis

The symbol sequences which are provided by the scanner are sequentially analysed by a syntax analyser or *parser*. Thus, the parser decides whether a certain sequence of symbols will be accepted by the considered programming language.

There are two main methods to do the syntactical analysis: *top-down parsing* and *bottom-up parsing*. The most efficient top-down and bottom-up parsers are based on so-called *LL-* and *LR-grammars*, respectively.

Top-down Analysis

When trying to find a derivation for a certain sentence it is possible to make a wrong decision, because there are probably different alternatives existing in a certain situation (i.e. informally spoken that the grammar was not exact enough). Therefore, we postulate the following rule for parsers:

> *For each production of the form*
> $$A \quad \rightarrow \quad \sigma_1 \mid \sigma_2 \mid ... \mid \sigma_n$$
> *we always should be able to choose the correct alternative for the generation of a parse tree.*

To fulfil this rule we need some additional information, i.e. we need to know

1) the set of all terminal symbols that may occur at the beginning of a sentence that can be derived from an arbitrary sequence of symbols;

2) the set of all terminal symbols that may follow after a nonterminal.

These are the so-called *FIRST* and *FOLLOW* sets.

Let G (N, T, P, S) be a grammar and α be an arbitrary sequence of symbols, thus
$\alpha \in (N \cup T)^*$. Then we define the set of terminals that can be the beginnings of any
derivable sentence as

$$\text{FIRST}(\alpha) \quad = \quad \{t \mid t \in T_\varepsilon \wedge \alpha \rightarrow^* t\alpha'\},$$

where $T_\varepsilon = T \cup \{\varepsilon\}$.

Let X be a nonterminal symbol. Then, FOLLOW(X) is the set of all terminal symbols
that can occur immediately to the right of X:

$$\text{FOLLOW}(X) \quad = \quad \{t \mid t \in T \wedge S \rightarrow^* \alpha X t \beta\}.$$

We call a context-free grammar G (N, T, P, S) an *LL(1)-grammar* if it has the following characteristics:

C1)   For each production
$$A \quad \rightarrow \quad \sigma_1 \mid \sigma_2 \mid ... \mid \sigma_n$$
it is required that
$$\text{FIRST}(\sigma_i) \cap \text{FIRST}(\sigma_j) = \varnothing \quad \forall i \neq j.$$

C2)   If the empty string ε can be derived from a nonterminal X, then it is required
that
$$\text{FIRST}(X) \cap \text{FOLLOW}(X) = \varnothing.$$

The first "L" of LL(1) means that the input will be read from left to right, while the
second "L" indicates leftmost derivations. The "1" means that we look ahead one
symbol at any step of the parse process.

Characteristic C1 means that for a given input string there exists just one possible
production at a certain state of the derivation, i.e. it will be obvious which alternative
of a production should be applied. Characteristic C2 helps to avoid so-called dead
ends occurring by (BNF-) productions of the form

$$A \quad \rightarrow \quad \{x\} \quad \text{or} \quad A \quad \rightarrow \quad [x]$$

where arbitrary occurrences (inclusive 0 times) are allowed (cf [TEUF 89]).

LL(1)-grammars are preferably used for top-down parsing. They allow an analysis with no dead ends, i.e. with no wrong decisions. An overview of general *top-down parsing* - which is often referred to as *recursive descent parsing* (or *predictive parsing*) - is given in the following.

Top-down analysis can be thought of as an attempt to find a leftmost derivation for a given input and in doing so to generate a parse tree from the top (i.e. the axiom of the grammar) down to the leaves of the tree. Thus, when analyzing an input, a top-down parser starts with the grammar's axiom. Then, as long as there are nonterminal leaves, one of the productions belonging to these leaves will be selected to generate the children of the nonterminal leaf, according to the right side of the selected production. An input is correct, if the sequence of the generated terminal leaves matches the sequence of input symbols.

This general method of recursive descent parsing can be applied not only to LL(1)-grammars, but only LL(1)-grammars will guarantee that no dead ends and therefore no backtracking will occur, this means that always a valid production for a nonterminal leaf will be selected (for examples see [TEUF 89]).

The most popular way to implement a recursive descent parser is to associate a procedure with each nonterminal of the grammar. Assume G (T, N, P, S) to be an LL(1)-grammar, where $N = \{N_0, N_1, N_2, ..., N_m\}$, $S = N_0$. The nonterminals correspond to the syntactical categories that should be recognized why they will be mapped to (recursive) procedures. When using an LL(1)-grammar the look ahead symbol (cf [AHOS 86] or [TEUF 89]) determines exactly the procedure called for each nonterminal and, thus, requires no backtracking. The parse tree is implicitly given by the sequence of procedure calls.

```
PROGRAM Parser;

  PROCEDURE Error (…);
  PROCEDURE N0;  . . .;
  PROCEDURE N1;  . . .;
  . . .
  PROCEDURE Nm;  . . .;

BEGIN
  Get_Symbol;
  N0;
END.
```

Fig. 2.5. Recursive descent parser structure

These procedures are embedded into a main program containing also an error-procedure and a procedure which provides the next symbol (Get_Symbol). The principle structure of a recursive descent parser for the above mentioned grammar G is shown in Figure 2.5.

Bottom-up Analysis

Like LL-grammars for top-down analysis we introduce LR-grammars in an informal way before starting to explain the principles of bottom-up parsing (shift-reduce analysis).

Context-free LR(k)-grammars are the largest class of grammars which can be parsed bottom-up. The "L" of LR(k) means that the input will be read from left to right, while the "R" indicates rightmost derivations. The "k" stands for a look ahead of k symbols.

We start with the fundamental definition of a *handle*. In general, we can say that a string's substring is called a handle, if it can be reduced using the left side of an appropriate production, provided that the reduction corresponds to a step in the leftmost reduction of the string to the grammars start symbol. Thus, a handle can informally said to be representing a particular reduction step (or derivation step, depending on the point of view). Clearly, handles (and therefore those reduction steps) can be recognized by the parsing technique which will be introduced later in this section.

Now, a more formal definition of a handle is given as follows: Let G (N, T, P, S) be a context-free grammar and suppose that

$$S \quad \rightarrow^* \quad \alpha Xt \quad \rightarrow \quad \alpha\beta t$$

is a rightmost derivation (where $t \in T^*$). Then, we call β at the explicitly shown position a *handle* of $\alpha\beta t$.

Thus, a substring β of a string $\alpha\beta t$ is said to be a handle if

$$\alpha\beta t \quad \leftarrow \quad \alpha Xt$$

is the leftmost reduction.

The processing of a sentence using leftmost reductions can be handled very comfortably when using a stack mechanism. Then, the handle will be always on top of the stack. Considering once again grammar G_0 (N_0, T_0, P_0, S_0), we are able to exemplify this as follows (where the changes on top of stack are caused either by pushing input symbols onto the stack or by reducing a handle on top of stack):

	input	stack
0	x + y - x	
1	x + y - x	**x**
2	+ y - x	**FACTOR**
3	+ y - x	**TERM**
4	+ y - x	EXPR
5	y - x	EXPR +
6	- x	EXPR + **y**
7	- x	EXPR + **FACTOR**
8	- x	**EXPR + TERM**
9	- x	EXPR
10	x	EXPR -
11		EXPR - **x**
12		EXPR - **FACTOR**
13		**EXPR - TERM**
14		EXPR

Here, the handle is bold faced. Reading the stack column from bottom to top we can recognize the rightmost derivation of the given sentence:

EXPR	→	EXPR - TERM
	→	EXPR - FACTOR
	→	EXPR - x
	→	EXPR + TERM - x
	→	EXPR + FACTOR - x
	→	EXPR + y - x
	→	TERM + y - x
	→	FACTOR + y - x
	→	x + y - x

The main actions using a stack are *shifting* and *reducing*, as shown in the above given example. This means, that one symbol from the input buffer is shifted onto the stack and if it is a handle it will be reduced to a nonterminal (i.e. the handle is replaced by the left side of an appropriate production).

Now, we define an LR(k)-grammar in the following (informal) way: A grammar is said to be an *LR(k)-grammar*, if it is always possible to determine the handle uniquely in consideration of the current stack contents and the next k input characters (this means that there will occur no shift-reduce and no reduce-reduce conflicts). The cases k = 0 and k = 1 are of practical interest.

LR(k)-grammars are *unambiguous*, otherwise it won't be possible to determine a handle uniquely. The proof is simple. We assume that G (N, T, P, S) is LR(k), for some k ≥ 0, and that w ∈ L (G). If

$$S \to^* w \quad = \quad S \to \sigma_1 \to \sigma_2 \to \ldots \to \sigma_{m-1} \to \sigma_m = w$$

is a rightmost derivation of w, then σ_{m-1} is unique since it corresponds to a uniquely determined handle (cf. the example above). (In other words, if

$$S \to \tau_1 \to \tau_2 \to \ldots \to \tau_{n-1} \to \tau_n = w$$

is a derivation according to G, then $\tau_{n-1} = \sigma_{m-1}$). Similarly, we conclude that the uniqueness of σ_k implies the uniqueness σ_{k-1}, for k = m, m-1, ... , 2. Therefore, it exists only one rightmost derivation of w and by that only one syntax tree and consequently only one leftmost derivation.

It can be shown that every LL(k)-grammar is also an LR(k)-grammar and that for every LR(k)-grammar with k > 1 exists an equivalent LR(1)-grammar (see for example [WAIT 84] or [SALO 73]).

Now, bottom-up parsing means to generate a parse tree for a given input starting at the leaves and working up to the root of the tree. This is equivalent to the leftmost reduction (or the rightmost derivation) of a sentence $\alpha \in T^*$ to the start symbol S of the considered grammar.

```
(* Assumptions: stack is empty and read-pointer is  *)
(*                on first input symbol               *)

Shift;   (* get first input symbol on stack *)

REPEAT
   IF   Handle_on_Top_of_Stack   THEN
      Reduce   (* replace top of stack by the left   *)
               (* side of a production               *)
   ELSE
      Shift    (* get next input symbol on stack     *)
   END;
UNTIL   Input_Empty AND No_Handle_on_Top_of_Stack;

IF   Axiom_on_Top_of_Stack   THEN
   Accept    (* input was syntactically correct   *)
ELSE
   Reject    (* input was syntactically incorrect *)
END;
```

Fig. 2.6. Algorithm for shift-reduce analysis

As we already mentioned the analysis of a sentence using leftmost reductions can be implemented using a stack. Then, the idea is that the sentence which should be analysed is shifted from an input buffer step by step onto the stack. Before each shift operation it is verified whether a handle is on top of the stack, which implies that it can be reduced using the left side of a production. The input will be accepted if the input buffer is empty and the axiom of the grammar is on the top of the stack. The principle algorithm is given in Figure 2.6.

We call this analysis *shift-reduce analysis* since the shift and reduce actions are characteristically to this analysis.

In the above given introduction to bottom-up parsing it was not explained how we decide whether to shift or to reduce in a specific situation (i.e. we gave no idea, how a handle can be recognized). The information needed for this decision process is being held in a so-called *action-table* and a *goto-table*. Then, the general LR-parsing model is given in Figure 2.7. This model consists of an analysing program, an input buffer, and the parse tables. The stack contains not only symbols of the grammar, but also states indicating the contents of the stack.

The state on top of the stack together with the current input symbol determines the above mentioned decision process, i.e. they index the parse table. Each state in the stack reflects uniquely the proceeding analysis process.

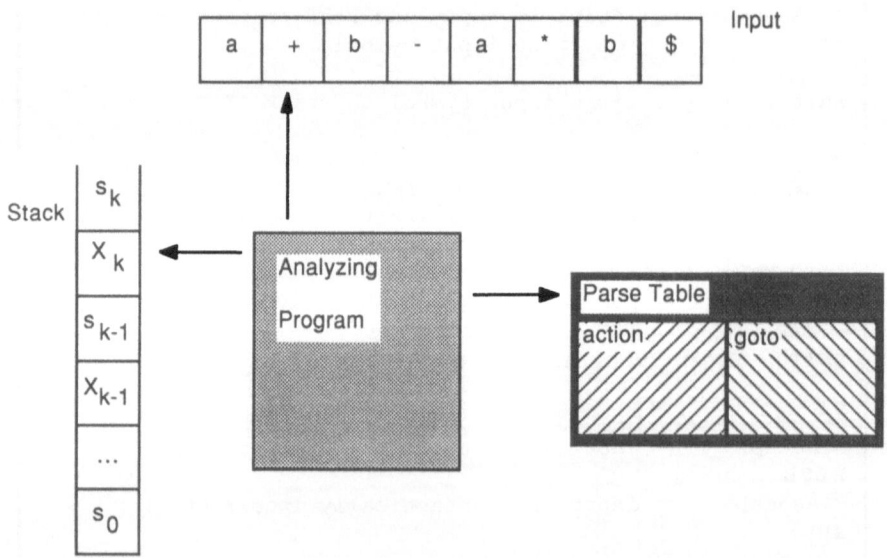

Fig. 2.7. Model of LR-parsing

```
(* initial state on stack,
   1st input sym. is next to read *)

WHILE   A[top_of_stack, current_input] ≠ accept   DO

  IF   A[top_of_stack, current_input] = shift(s)   THEN

    push(current_input);
    push(s);   (* s is new top of stack *)
    INC(read_pointer);

  ELSIF   A[top_of_stack, current_input] = reduce(p)   THEN
                  (* p is the number of a production *)

    h := length(handle);
    FOR   i := 1   TO   2*h   DO   pop(…);
                    (* pop h symbols of the grammar *)
                    (*    and h states off the stack *)
    s := G[top_of_stack, left_side(p)];
                    (* get the new top of stack    *)
                    (* from the goto-table          *)
    push(left_side(p));
    push(s);

  ELSIF   A[top_of_stack, current_input] = empty   THEN

    Error(…);

  END;

END;
```

Fig. 2.8. Algorithm for LR-parsing

As we have already seen when discussing the general shift-reduce analysis, the principle actions of the parser or analysing program are

- *shift*, i.e. the next input symbol will be shifted onto the stack and depending on that symbol and the current stack a new state will get on top of stack;

- *reduce*, i.e. a handle is recognized (considering the current input symbol and the state on top of stack) and is reduced using left side of a production; depending on that symbol and the current state, a new state will get on top of stack;

- *accept*, i.e. the input will be accepted when the end of the input is reached and a final state is on top of stack;

- *error*, otherwise.

These actions of the parser are supported by the parse table, i.e. the *action-table* and the *goto-table*. The principle algorithm is given in Figure 2.8.

The construction of the parse tables is not a trivial task and the explanation of the appropriate mechanisms is beyond the scope of this text. For more detailed information and examples see [AHOS 86] or [TEUF 89].

Semantic Analysis

Lexical as well as syntactical analysis are not concerned with the *semantic meaning* of programs. But a compiler has to check not only the syntactical correctness of a given source code, it has also to check, whether the semantics correspond to that of the programming language. This means that *semantic analysis* has to guarantee that all *context sensitive rules* of a programming language are considered.

An example of such a context-sensitive rule of a programming language is that in languages like PASCAL or MODULA-2 identifiers have to be declared before they are used. *Symbol tables* are used to check if an identifier was already declared. In general the semantic analysis of a compiler uses the information of the syntax analysis together with the semantic rules of the programming language to generate an *internal representation* of the source code which should be compiled. This generation of an internal representation means that the compiler has to interpret the meaning of the source code and, therefore, that the compiler semantically analyzes the syntactical structures of the source code as they are recognized by the scanner and parser. The internal representation is an *intermediate code* which will be passed to the code generator. The most popular intermediate codes are

- postfix notation,

- three-address code, and

- two-address code.

Code Generation

The function of a code generator is basicly the translation of the output from the syntax and semantic analysis (i.e. the intermediate code) into an equivalent sequence of instructions which can be executed on the target machine. Two essential requirements exist for the output of a code generator:

- the produced code *must be correct*, and

- the code *should be optimal.*

Clearly, the first requirement is a necessity, while the second requirement cannot be reached fully (in general). Since the generation of optimal code is a NP-complete problem, it is possible to generate high quality code, but not necessarily optimal code.

When generating machine code on the basis of an intermediary code it can be assumed that all necessary semantic checks were carried out. That means that type checking and most of all type conversion has already taken place and, therefore, that the code generator must not take care about all the semantic rules of the programming language. But the conclusion can by no means be that code generation is an easy process. In general two basic decisions must take place when generating code.

- *Allocating Registers*: Since processors and language implementations often require that specific registers (or even/odd register-pairs) must be used for certain purposes, register allocation is a non-trivial task. For example, some machines separate general-purpose registers from index registers, and others may require the operands for certain instructions in even/odd register-pairs.

- *Selecting Instructions*: It is often possible that several computations can be done in different ways. To choose the best (i.e. 'optimal') sequence of instructions usually requires contextual knowledge which makes this decision non-trivial. A simple example is, to choose an increment instruction (if available) instead of a sequence of MOV and ADD instructions, when incrementing a variable by one.

Additionally to these two basic decisions which are common to nearly all code generators, a few other important things must be decided when generating code for a target hardware. Among them are the selection of the addressing mode as well as fixing the order of evaluation. For instance, the instruction set of a target machine probably allows just a subset of all possible addressing modes, as the ADD instruction of the *Motorola 68000* processor, which does not allow memory-to-memory addition (i.e. either the source or the destination of this instruction must be a data register). Thus, the selected addressing mode may limit the available instructions in a certain case.

2.4   Run-time Environments

Different programming languages require different environments for the execution of programs. The allocation and deallocation of data objects and their representation must be handled at run-time; the activation or execution of procedures (or program units, in general) must also be managed at run-time (e.g. in the case of recursive procedures several activations might be alive at the same time).

The languages differ in their run-time environments depending on the features they provide. For example, FORTRAN does not allow recursively defined procedures or data structures and, therefore, the memory requirements for any FORTRAN program can be determined at compile time. This is not possible in languages such as ALGOL 60, PASCAL or MODULA-2, since they allow recursively defined structures which require dynamic memory allocation techniques. However, those languages usually combine stack allocation and heap allocation techniques.

Storage Organization

Assuming that the compiler can use a particular block of memory for a compiled program, then the run-time storage might be organized as shown in Figure 2.9. The *code section* contains the generated machine instructions. The size of this section can be fixed at compile time. The size of some of the data objects may also be known at compile time and, therefore, they can also be placed in a fixed memory location, the *static data section*. Such data objects exist during the whole lifetime of the program. All these locations can be statically allocated since they do not change during program execution. The advantage of statically allocated data objects is obvious: their addresses can be coded into the machine instructions.

The *stack* is used to handle the activations of different program units (e.g. procedures). The information which is needed to execute a program unit is stored in so-called *activation records* (see below). The activation of a program unit causes the interruption of the currently executed program unit and its actual status is saved on the stack, which then can be restored after the termination of the called unit.

The *heap* is that storage area which in languages, such as PASCAL, is used to allocate memory for data objects (or program units) which are generated during run-time in an unpredictable way, i.e. in cases where the number and lifetime of such objects cannot be represented by a static activation structure. The size of both, stack and heap, can change during program execution which is represented in Figure 2.9 by their opposite position. Both can grow towards each other.

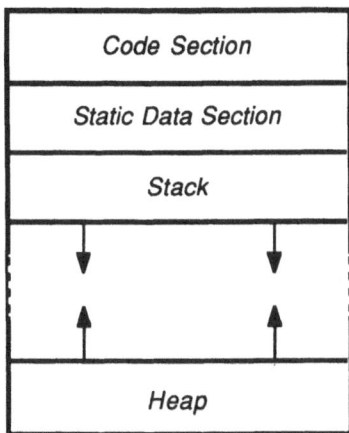

Fig. 2.9. Typical organization of the run-time storage

Activation Records

Program units usually need some information for their execution. All this information is treated as a data block which is called *activation record*. An activation record
is pushed onto the run-time stack when a procedure or, generally speaking, a program unit is called (i.e. activated), and it is popped off the stack when the procedure
is terminated. A procedure's activation record could consist of the following information:

- *Local data*: That data which is local to the execution of a procedure.

- *Parameters and results*: Space for actual parameters and possible results.

- *Machine status*: Information about the machine status just before the procedure call, e.g. values of the program counter and registers. This information must be restored when terminating the procedure.

- *Static links*: A link to the actually accessible non-local variables. It is
  given by the base address of the data area forming the environment of
  the program unit. The methods used are called *static link* or *display* (see
  [AHOS 86], for example). FORTRAN, for instance, does not need this information, because all non-local data are stored in the static data section.

- *Dynamic link*: A link to the activation record of the calling instance. This
  control link is given as the base address of that activation record and it is
  used to reorganize the stack when terminating a procedure.

Storage Allocation Techniques

We distinguish between three different allocation techniques:

- static allocation,

- stack allocation, and

- heap allocation.

Using *static storage allocation* techniques the data objects are bound to their memory locations at compile time. This technique can be applied, if the compiler knows exactly the number of all objects, as well as the type and therefore the size of all objects. Obviously, languages using static storage allocation do not allow either dynamic data structures nor do they allow recursive procedure calls.

A *stack* is that storage organization which is used by most programming languages. The stack is used for holding the activation records of program units. The dynamic allocation and deallocation is achieved by pushing the activation records onto the stack or popping them off the stack.

Heap allocation is another method of dynamic storage management. Pointers can be used to access dynamically storage from a separate part of the run-time memory, called heap. In different programming languages certain ways to require heap allocation for dynamic data structures exist. For example, in MODULA-2 or PASCAL the *new* and *dispose* procedures are available for the programmer to explicitly allocate and deallocate storage during the run-time. In other languages - like SNOBOL or LISP - storage allocation and deallocation might be implicit, e.g. the usage of variable length character strings in SNOBOL. Heap management can become rather complex, since it is possible to allocate and deallocate storage in any order. Therefore, strategies to manage and combine free storage blocks are necessary.

These techniques introduced in this Section are explained in more detail in the following Chapters when discussing certain implementation techniques.

3 Data Types

A *data type* is a set of data objects together with an appropriate set of operations for the object's manipulation. Programs are usually written to perform certain actions and, in doing so, to manipulate some kind of data objects in certain ways. Thus, the possibilities of data representation by the features of a programming language are very important for a programmer. Programming languages partly differ from each other by the allowed *types of data* and the appropriate *operations* on data objects of these types.

The subject of this Chapter is to discuss the specification of data types and the concept of binding, followed by an introductory to elementary data types, structured data types, as well as abstract data types. Type checking, the implementation of data types and a consideration of variables - the carriers of certain types - will finally close this Chapter.

3.1   Specifications

Data objects on the physical level of a computer can be seen just as a sequence of bits with no distinction between the meaning of the different objects. The introduction of types allows a classification of data objects on a higher level which, then, can be projected onto lower levels by the compiler. The classification of data objects is the same as in mathematics where we classify variables according to certain characteristics. In mathematics we distinguish between integer, real and complex variables, for example. We specify spaces for the variables of these types and we declare certain operators and functions on these types. Thus, data classification in computing is closely related to those classification methods in mathematics.

In programming languages we can distinguish between different type levels which from the user's point of view form a hierarchy of complexity, i.e. each level allows new data types or operations of greater complexity. These levels are (cf Figure 3.1):

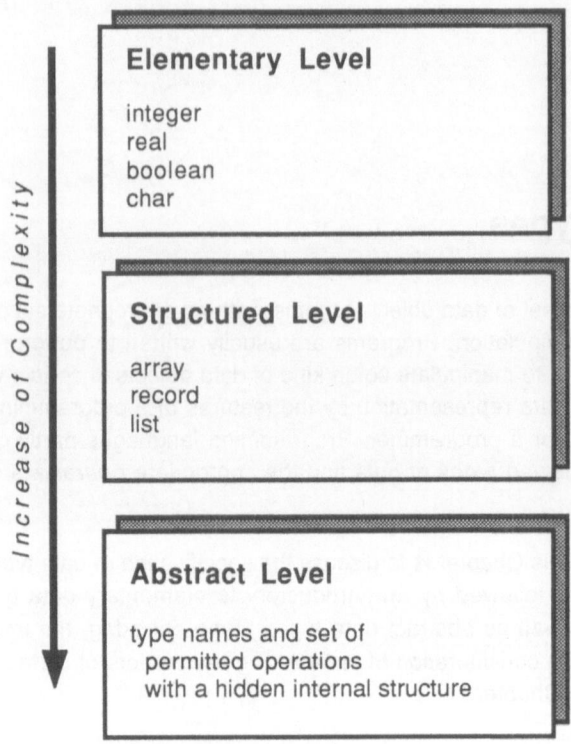

Fig. 3.1. Type levels in programming languages

- *Elementary level*: Elementary (sometimes also called basic or simple) types, such as *integers*, *reals*, *booleans*, and *characters*, are supported by nearly every programming language. Data objects of these types can be manipulated by well known operators, like +, −, *, or /, on the programming level. It is the task of the compiler to translate the operators onto the correct machine instructions, e.g. fixed-point and floating-point operations.

- *Structured level*: Most high level programming languages allow the definition of structured types which are based on simple types. We distinguish between *static* and *dynamic* structures. Static structures are *arrays*, *records*, and *sets*, while dynamic structures are a bit more complicated, since they are recursively defined and may vary in size and shape during the execution of a program. *Lists* and *trees* are dynamic structures.

- *Abstract level*: Programmer defined abstract data types are a *set of data objects* with *declared operations* on these data objects. The implementation or internal representation of abstract data types is *hidden* to the users of these types to avoid uncontrolled manipulation of the data objects (i.e the concept of *encapsulation*).

Now, specifying a data type means to define the type's *characteristics*, its *value range*, as well as its *operations* (cf Figure 3.2). Obviously, a good *name* for a type must also be found to refer to these entities. The characteristics of a type specify certain properties which data objects (e.g. variables) of that type have, e.g. if the objects have a fixed-point representation or a floating-point representation. Thus, the characteristics of a data type determine the representation of that type on the computer.

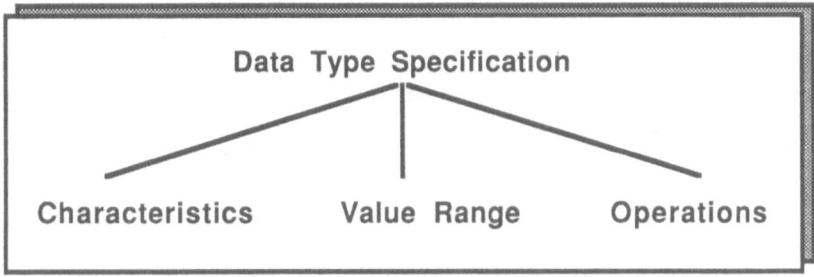

Fig. 3.2. Specification of data types

In mathematics we are used to have a clear defined range of values for a specific type, even if this range is infinite. However, on a computer we won't find an infinite range of values for a data type, but we have to establish the set of all possible values which can be taken by a data object of a specific type. For example, the type *integer* provides a subrange of all integers, which is usually determined by the greatest and least integer that can be represented on a certain hardware. For elementary data types the range of values is given by a set with a order relation declared on this set, i.e. for any two elements x and y of the set, either $x \le y$ or $y \le x$.

For the manipulation of data objects of a specific type we have to define certain operators. Again, we find a close relationship to mathematics. Analogically to mathematical functions, a domain and a range is defined for each operator, and the operator describes a mapping from the domain (or the operator's arguments) onto the range (or the operator's appropriate result). This mapping can be given as an algorithm.

Considering operators, such as +, −, *, /, we know that the meaning of these operators depends on their context; we call this *overloading*. For example, both integer and real addition are simply expressed by +. It is the task of the compiler to determine the types of the arguments and, then, choosing the correct machine instructions. Thus, it is impounded that, for instance, *integer + integer* results in an *integer* and *real + real* in a *real*.

By the last example we implied also the *conversion* of types when considering *integer + real*, for example. We should not forget such problems when specifying a data type. Two methods of type conversion exist: *Implicit conversion* and *explicit conversion*. For example, PASCAL allows the multiplication of a real with an integer data object and the conversion is implicitly done by the compiler. Not so MODULA-2, here we have (i.e. the programmer has) to convert explicitly the integer variable into a real variable before the multiplication can be executed.

3.2   The Concept of Binding

With constants, variables, expressions, functions (procedures), or language entities in general are usually certain properties, or attributes, associated. Examples of those properties are names, types, memory location, or number, type, and passing mechanisms for parameters. The association of a set of such properties to an entity of a language is called *binding*.

We distinguish between *static* and *dynamic* binding according to when the binding occurs: Dynamic binding is done and can be changed during run-time, while static binding is done before run-time and is not changed during the program execution. Bindings can take place at different times:

- *Language definition time*: Certain features of a programming language are bound to appropriate attributes during the language definition time. For example, in ALGOL-like programming languages the well known operators +, −, *, / are usually bound to sets of addition operations, subtraction operations, multiplication operations, and division operations.

- *Language implementation time*: A compiler writer normally can decide about special aspects of a programming language according to the possibilities of the target hardware. For example, if a floating-point processor with defined roundings is available, code should be generated to use this processor.

- *Compile time*: Explicitly or implicitly declared variables are bound to the appropriate types during compile time. For example, PASCAL variables are bound to particular (e.g. user-defined) data types at compile time.

- *Run-time*: At run-time we find bindings of variables to their values or memory locations. But we can also find a type binding at run-time. In this case, a variable's type is not specified by a declaration of the variable, but by the assignment of a value, i.e. the value´s type determines the variable's type, and the type can change with another assignment. For example, in APL a variable A is of type integer after the execution of the assignment statement A ← 10, after the execution of A ← 10.1, A is a floating-piont variable.

The most important disadvantage of programming languages allowing dynamic type binding is a higher probability of errors during program execution, since the compiler cannot check whether, for instance, certain assignments are correct. Dynamic type binding contradicts the concept of *strong typing* which goes along with the discussion about the so-called structured programming. The concept of strong typing stands for the statically type binding of each variable and the possibility of static (or at least dynamic) type checkings. Thus, most of the possible errors are early recognizable at compile time.

3.3   Elementary Data Types

We find in each programming language a set of *elementary* (or so-called *built-in*) *data types*. Although the sets are slightly different from language to language, the types

- *integer*,

- *real*,

- *boolean*, and

- *char*

can be found in nearly every (imperative) language. Since the numeric data types are highly dependent on the hardware representation of the numbers and the implementation of the arithmetic, their usage can cause different results on different computers.

Integer

Integer is the simplest numeric data type of the built-in types of programming languages. Usually integers are represented in a word or a set of words of the computer, where the leftmost bit indicates the sign. For example, an 8-bit word can be used to represent values in the range −128 to + 127, using the 2's complement. Thus, the word length of the computer determines the range of integer values (cf Table 3.1).

Table 3.1.   Ranges of integer values

Word Length	Range
8	−128 to +127
16	−32768 to +32767
32	−2147483648 to +2147483647
64	-2^{63} to $2^{63} - 1$
N	-2^{N-1} to $2^{N-1} - 1$

We are often allowed to define *long integers* to enlarge the value range of the integers. In this case integers are represented by two or more words. The basic arithmetic operations on data objects of type integer are mapped onto the hardware's fixed-point arithmetic operations.

Real

The data type real is used to model real numbers. In contrast to the data type integer, where we can represent each integer number within a range, the representation of each real number within a certain range is not possible. In mathematics, for example, $\sqrt{2}$ is exact and we can work with this real number. But on a computer this real number cannot be correctly represented (the same counts for such important numbers like π or *e*).

The representation of real numbers and most of all the operations on real numbers are an awkward task. The basic operations, such as addition and multiplication, must be done with well-defined roundings, i.e. a computer arithmetic must be based on a mathematical theory [KULI 81], [TEUF 84]. Unfortunately, there exist a great number of computers where these requirements are not considered. Therefore, serious problems can occur when executing a program on another hardware.

To overcome the problems with different floating-point representations on different computers, the IEEE Computer Society has developed a proposed standard for floating-point representation and arithmetic [IEEE 82]. The IEEE floating-point format is given in Figure 3.3 (64-bit format). It shows the elements which are common to all floating-point or real number representations: The sign of the mantissa, the mantissa itself (i.e. the fractional part of a real number), and the exponent, which is often biased (i.e. a fixed value, called the bias, is subtracted from the exponent to get the true exponent value, thus, exponent values in the range 1 to 254 can represent actual exponents in the range −126 to +127, for example). Floating-point numbers are typically represented in a *normalized* form, this means that the leftmost bit of the mantissa is always 1 (and, therefore, is usually not stored).

Sign	Exponent	Mantissa
0 1	11 12	63

Fig. 3.3.   IEEE floating-point format

As for integers, most of the programming languages provide data types, such as *long real*. With long reals we have a larger mantissa (e.g. double the length), but this does not mean that we automatically get an increase of accuracy for all computations. The problems and risks with insufficient implemented computer arithmetic are obvious.

Boolean

The boolean data type is the simplest built-in data type of (imperative) programming languages. Its value range consists of only two elements: *true* and *false*. Standard operations bound on the boolean data type are the logical operations *and*, *or*, and *not*. For the comparison of boolean values we usually find *false* considered to be less than *true* (e.g. in PASCAL, MODULA-2, etc.). Obviously, boolean data objects theoretically can be represented by a single bit. But the values are bound to the smallest addressable element which is normally a byte. The operations are also bound to certain machine operations.

Character

The value range of the data type char (or character) is bound to a set of characters which can be a defined enumeration or a standard set, which, then, is mostly the ASCII character set. ASCII (American Standard Code for Information Interchange) stands not only for a character set, but also for a code allowing the representation of characters by a sequence of bits. The ASCII character set contains not only the digits and the elements of the alphabet, but also a number of control characters. Each character of the ASCII character set is represented by a unique 7-bit pattern. Thus, the representation of char data objects is usually given by bytes (8 bit), where the eighth bit is either unused or used as a parity bit. Another standard code which is mainly used on IBM computers is the 8-bit code EBCDIC (Extended Binary Coded Decimal Interchange Code).

An order is defined on the character sets, usually the alphabetic order. This order determines the relational operators, such as <, ≤, =, ≥, >, which are bound to the data type *char*.

3.4   Structured Data Types

The previously introduced built-in data types allow only the representation of the basic elements of the real world. But real world problems normally require a more structured way of defining data. Imperative programming languages, such as PASCAL, MODULA-2, or ADA, allow for this reason the definition of *user defined* (structured) types applying the concept of *orthogonality*. This means that – on the bases of some elementary constructs – flexible composing mechanisms are available. The definition of such structured data types is mainly based on well-known mathematical composing methods, like

- ordered schema of elements, e.g. vectors and matrices,

- cartesian products, or

- sets.

In this way the elementary data types can be used to define data objects with a higher complexity, i.e. as an aggregate (or unit) of elementary objects. Modern programming languages normally allow the naming of such complex structures. Thus, the programmer can define type names for aggregations of elementary or user-defined types, and thereafter, he can declare arbitrary variables or data objects to be of this type (similar to the declaration of simple type data objects).

Vectors and Arrays

An *array* is an ordered pattern of homogeneous elements (i.e. elements of the same type). Specific data objects are accessed by an index which is relative to the first element. Arrays can be multi-dimensional; one-dimensional arrays are sometimes called *vectors*. An array declaration usually specifies

- the array's name,

- the index range and type,

- the type of the elements.

For example the MODULA-2 declaration

```
VAR   a :   ARRAY [0..9] OF REAL;
```

defines a one-dimensional array of name a, the elements of which are of type real and the index range is a subrange of the integers, i.e. the index of the first array element is 0 and that of the last element is 9. The access of an array element (in MODULA-2, other languages may use a slightly different syntax) is given by

    a[k]

where k is an element of the subrange [0..9]. Several programming languages allow for the index range not only subranges of the integer values, but a subrange of any enumeration type.

An interesting question is, whether the array bounds should be constant during a program execution, or whether they can be changed dynamically. While in PASCAL array bounds are constants, ADA or SIMULA 67, for instance, allow dynamic indexing ranges. Obviously, constant array sizes are simpler to implement than dynamic ones which need more expensive dynamic storage allocation techniques.

The implementation of fixed-size arrays is not very difficult, since the size of the array is known at compile-time. The access to an element a[k] of a one-dimensional array a[l1..u1] is given by the address

$$base_a + (k - l1) * size,$$

where $base_a$ denotes the address of the first element of the array (i.e. a[l1]) in the data area, l1 (u1) denotes the lower (upper) bound of the array, and size is the size of storage (counted in words or bytes), which must be allocated to store a single element of the array (depending on the array's type, of course).

Since the storage of a computer is normally one-dimensional, multi-dimensional arrays must be mapped onto a linear structure to store them. This can be done in

- *row-major* form, or

- *column-major* form.

a [3, 2]
a [3, 3]
a [3, 4]
a [3, 5]
a [4, 2]
a [4, 3]
a [4, 4]
a [4, 5]

Fig. 3.4. Row-major form to store a two-dimensional array

Row-major form means that the array elements are stored with the rightmost index varying the most rapidly, while in column-major form the array elements are stored with the leftmost index varying the most rapidly. Figure 3.4 shows a two-dimensional array a[3..4, 2..5] stored in row-major form.

The address of an element a[i, j] of a two-dimensional array a[l1..u1, l2..u2] is then given for row-major forms as

$$base_a + ((i - l1) * (u2 - l2 + 1) + (j - l2)) * size ,$$

and for column-major forms as

$$base_a + ((j - l2) * (u1 - l1 + 1) + (i - l1)) * size .$$

In the case, where both lower bounds are 0, these address formulas can be simplified to

$$base_a + (i * (u2 + 1) + j) * size$$
and

$$base_a + (j * (u1 + 1) + i) * size,$$

respectively.

Using these formulas, we can determine the address of the array element a [4, 4] (cf Figure 3.4) as

$$
\begin{aligned}
adr\ (a[4,4]) &= base_a + ((4 - 3) * (5 - 2 + 1) + (4 - 2)) * size \\
&= base_a + 6 * size
\end{aligned}
$$

for row-major form, and

$$
\begin{aligned}
adr\ (a[4,4]) &= base_a + ((4 - 2) * (4 - 3 + 1) + (4 - 3)) * size \\
&= base_a + 5 * size
\end{aligned}
$$

for column-major form.

The handling of dynamic arrays (i.e. arrays where the upper and/or lower bounds, and hence the size, of the array are only known at run-time) is a bit more complicated. In general, the problem is solved by generating an array descriptor at compile-time, which then is initialized at run-time. The descriptor reserves space to hold the information about the array (e.g. number of dimension, upper and lower bounds), while space for the array elements itself is allocated form the heap during program execution. The addressing of the elements of a dynamic array is the same as for fixed-size arrays, but the upper and lower bounds must be taken from the descriptor.

Records

While an array forms an aggregate of homogeneous objects, *records* are aggregates of maybe heterogeneous data objects. Records (in PASCAL, MODULA-2 etc., or *structures* in ALGOL 68, or C) are based on the idea of the cartesian product of sets: If X_1, X_2, ..., X_n are non-empty sets, then their product $X_1 \times X_2 \times ... \times X_n$ is the set of all ordered n-tuples $(x_1, x_2, ..., x_n)$, where x_i is an element of the set X_i for each subscript i. The components of a record are called *fields*; each field has its own distinct name. A record declaration usually specifies

- the record's name,

- the names and types of the fields.

For example, the MODULA-2 declaration

```
TYPE    NGFreqs  =   RECORD
                        ng : ARRAY [1..6] OF CHAR;
                        tf : CARDINAL;
                        rf : REAL
                     END;
VAR     ngram : NGFreqs;
```

defines a record of name NGFreqs, the elements of which are of type real, cardinal, and an array of characters. Then, the type NGFreqs is instantiated by declaring the variable ngram. The access to an element (say rf) of this structure (in MODULA-2, again other languages may use a slightly different syntax) is given by

```
ngram.rf ,
```

i.e. the selection of record components is done by names which are known at compile time. This is different to the selection of array elements, where the index is normally calculated during the program execution. This form of referencing a component of a record is called *qualified name form* and is used in PASCAL, MODULA-2, and ADA, for example. ALGOL 68 is an example for a language which references components by the so-called *functional notation*, e.g. ngram(rf).

Obviously, records can also be defined to be an aggregate of homogeneous objects, as the following example for the definition of complex numbers shows:

```
TYPE    complex  =   RECORD
                        re, im : REAL
                     END;
```

The implementation of records is fairly simple and very similar to fixed-size arrays. A record's size is known at compile time and the access to a field of a record, say r.k, can be done via a base address ($base_r$) and an appropriate offset:

$$base_r + \sum_{i=1}^{k-1} size(r.i) \; ,$$

where size(r.i) is the size of the i-th component of r.

Variant Records

Variant records are specified to have a choice between different, alternative structures. They are used to structure the data objects of problems which have a great many elements in common and differ in certain components, or, for example, if problems can be structured in different ways. An example for the latter is a type defining figures that can be either circles or rectangles:

```
TYPE  Figures  =  RECORD
                     CASE kind:(circle,rect) OF
                          circle: r: REAL;
                        | rect: l, w: REAL
                     END
                  END;
```

The component which determines the variant actually used (in our example kind) is called type discriminator or tag field. In the given example a circle is given by its radius, and a rectangle by its length and width. The implementation of variant records is in general straightforward, i.e. storage space is allocated for the largest possible variant.

Two major problems exist with PASCAL and MODULA-2 variant records. First it is possible to omit the tag from the variant record which makes it impossible to determine the current variant type. Thus, improper assignments become possible. The other problem is that a program can change the tag, without changing the variant in an appropriate way. This leads to inconsistent states and, therefore, can cause run-time errors.

Pointer

A *pointer* is a reference to an object and, thus, it provides indirect access to data objects, i.e. the value of a pointer variable is either a valid memory address of a data object or nil, indicating that the pointer references no data object. Two concepts can be observed:

- Pointers reference to objects of the type to which the pointer is bound.

- Pointers reference to objects of any type.

The first of these concepts can be found, for example, in PASCAL, MODULA-2, or ADA. Pointers are only allowed to reference data objects of a single type, which is determined with a pointer's declaration. The binding of a type to a pointer variable distinguishes high level language pointers from addresses in assembly languages. This binding has the advantage that a strong typing concept (and, therefore, static type checking) can be applied. In MODULA-2, for example, a pointer declaration can be given in the following way:

```
TYPE   NGFptr  =  POINTER TO NGFreqs;
```

defining a pointer to data objects of the above defined structured type `NGFreqs` which consists of a character array, a cardinal, and a real field.

The concept that a pointer can reference data objects of any kind can be found in SNOBOL4 or PL/1, for example. Static type checking is impossible if a pointer is not restricted to reference data objects only of a single type. This increases the probability for unreliable program structures using pointers. Therefore, modern high level programming languages are mostly based on the concept that pointer variables are bound to a single type.

By the introduction of pointer types it becomes possible to define recursive data structures which are much more flexible, since they can vary in size. Such a recursive definition is shown in the following example (in MODULA-2 notation):

```
TYPE   NGFptr   =  POINTER TO NGFreqs;
       NGFreqs  =  RECORD
                      ng : ARRAY [1..6] OF CHAR;
                      tf : CARDINAL;
                      rf : REAL;
                      left, right : NGFptr
                   END;
VAR   NgramTree :  NGFptr;
```

Now, `NgramTree` is defined as a pointer to a binary tree whose nodes contain a real and a cardinal object, and a character array, as well as two pointers pointing to a left and right successor of the node (or to nil). An empty tree is generated by

```
NgramTree := nil;
```

One characteristic of recursive data structures is the ability to vary in size and, thus, that a compiler cannot statically allocate storage for the components of such structures. The compiler allocates only memory to store the value, i.e. an address, of the pointer variable. Storage for the structure to which the pointer points is allocated dynamically during program execution, i.e. whenever a new element of such a structure is to be generated, memory is dynamically allocated from a storage area, which is usually called a *heap*. For this, we normally find an intrinsic function like

```
new(NgramTree);
```

This statement effectively allocates storage for a record of type NGFreqs and initializes the pointer value by the address (absolute or relative) of the data object (i.e. a dynamic variable).

Pointers can be used to reference either to the contents of the memory location to which the pointer variable itself is bound (i.e. an address), or it can be used to reference to the contents of the memory location whose address is the contents of the location to which the pointer variable is bound. We call the latter *pointer dereferencing*. In MODULA-2 or PASCAL dereferencing is done using the symbol "^", e.g. NgramTree^.

The concept of dereferencing is shown in Figure 3.5, where the address of the pointer variable NgramTree is assumed to be 1000 and its value to be 2000. A normal reference to NgramTree yields 2000, while a dereferenced reference allows access to the contents of the memory location with the address 2000, e.g.

```
NgramTree^.ng := 'abcdef';
```

writes the string 'abcdef' into this location. Obviously, we have to use some offsets to address the different fields of the structure. The assignments

```
NgramTree^.tf     := 0;
NgramTree^.rf     := 0.0;
NgramTree^.left  := nil;
NgramTree^.right := nil;
```

will initialize the rest of the node which was generated by the above *new* operation. Figure 3.6 shows the according binary tree after these assignments.

Along with the *new* operation we find usually a *dispose* operation to return explicitly allocated memory dynamically (in languages like MODULA-2 or PASCAL). For example (again in MODULA-2 syntax),

```
dispose(NgramTree);
```

returns the memory pointed to by NgramTree to the storage pool. The value of the pointer variable becomes undefined and the data formerly associated with NgramTree^ are no longer accessible. The memory returned to the storage pool can then be reused later when another *new* operation is executed. In other languages – like SNOBOL4 or LISP – storage allocation and deallocation might be implicit, e.g. the usage of variable length character strings in SNOBOL4.

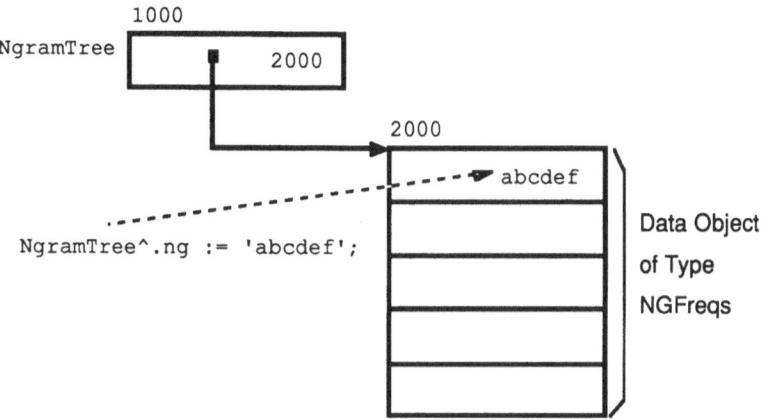

Fig. 3.5. Assignment NgramTree^.ng := 'abcdef

The availability of deallocation operations for dynamic variables in a programming language means that a great part of the storage management must be done by the programmer. This is the reason why major problems can occur when using pointer variables: After using the dispose operation the programmer must remember that the pointer variable no longer points to anything meaningful. We call the case where a pointer points to a dynamic variable which has been deallocated (i.e. which is no longer meaningful) a *dangling pointer*.

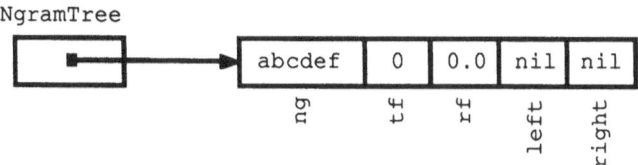

Fig. 3.6. A one element tree

The *new* and *dispose* operation for the allocation or deallocation of memory are the critical issues in the implementation associated with pointers. Dynamic storage allocation techniques are required along with a storage management system (for more details see Chapter 3.7).

Sets

Set types in programming languages are based on set theory. As in mathematics, a *set* is an unordered collection of distinct elements of a base type B (which usually must be a scalar or subrange type). In MODULA-2, for instance, we can define a set type on the bases of a qualified identifier, an enumeration type, or a subrange type, e.g.

```
TYPE    Digits   =   [0..9];
        DigitSet =   SET OF Digits;
VAR     even, odd:   DigitSet;
```

defines a set type `DigitSet` based on the subrange type `Digits`, as well as the two set variables `even` and `odd`.

The possible values of a set variable are the elements of the *powerset* of the base type B. The set of all subsets of a given set B is called the powerset of B. This powerset contains B itself, the void set $\emptyset$, and – if B's cardinality is greater than 1 –

$$2^{\text{cardinality}(B)} - 2$$

subsets S, satisfying

$$\emptyset \subset S \subset B, \quad S \neq \emptyset, \quad \text{and} \quad S \neq B.$$

For instance, the powerset of of a set {a, b, c} has the six subsets {a}, {b}, {c}, {a, b}, {a, c}, and {b, c}. Set variables are usually, like other variables, initially undefined. The MODULA-2 assignment statement

```
even := DigitSet {2, 4, 6};
```

assigns the appropriate set to the variable `even`.

The basic operations which are bound to set types are the following:

- *Set intersection* ("*"): The intersection of two sets $S_1 * S_2$ is the set of all those elements common to both S_1 and S_2.

- *Set union* ("+"): The union of two sets $S_1 + S_2$ is the set of all those elements which belong either to $S1$ or to S_2 (or to both).

- *Set difference* ("–"): The difference of two sets $S_1 - S_2$ is the set of all those elements which belong to $S1$ but not to S_2.

- *Set membership*: Tests if a certain value is an element of a set.

- *Set insertion*: Inserts a value in a set, provided that the value is not already an element of the set.

- *Set deletion*: Deletes an element of a set.

Often there is no maximum size of the cardinality of a set defined by the language (like in PASCAL or MODULA-2), but the implementations of these languages usually define limits for the size of sets, which can be quite small (e.g. the number of bits in a word or a small multiple of words). This makes the implementation of set types as bit strings very simple. Then, the operations on sets are usually directly supported by the hardware.

Procedure Types

Although procedure types do not appear in any of the common procedural languages – except in MODULA-2 – they should be introduced here, since they represent a very powerful concept. The introduction of a procedure data type allows the consideration of procedures, like data values, as objects that may be assigned to variables. A *procedure type* declaration specifies

- the number of parameters of procedures (or functions) of that type;

- the types and variable or value status of the parameters of procedures (or functions) of that type;

- the type of the result, in case of functions.

For example, we define a procedure type P1 with two cardinal value parameters and one real variable parameter in MODULA-2 in the following way:

```
TYPE    P1 = PROCEDURE (CARDINAL, CARDINAL, VAR REAL);
```

Any procedure with such a parameter structure is of type P1. Variables of this type can be declared and assignments can be made to such variables. A procedure variable can be called (or activated) in exactly the same way as the procedure itself. But the major use of procedure types is to enable the passing of procedures or functions as parameters. This can be very important in certain situations where different procedures are required to operate on similar contexts.

File Types

A *file* is a structure of data objects belonging logically together. Major aspects of files are:

- A file's lifetime must not depend on a program's lifetime.

- A file is usually located on a secondary storage (such as a disk or a tape).

- A file might be accessed by different programs.

Files are still *this* medium for the I/O of huge amounts of data and they can act as a communication link between different applications. Programming languages normally provide a *file type* to perform the management of files, i.e. the creation, the read/write access, and the deletion of files. Along with these operations we often find operations to open and close a file, and to specify a file's access attributes. Such access attributes are read-only, write-only, or read-write.

Normally, the implementation of files depends on what is supported by the operating system and, of course, what kind of secondary storage is used. Several structures of file organizations are known, e.g.:

- *Sequential files*, the simplest, but probably most important structure. The components of a sequential file can be accessed only in linear order, i.e. at any time only a single component of the file is accessible. The component is specified by the current position of the access mechanism. Since secondary storage still depends on some forms of mechanical movement – the basic characteristic of which is a sequential behaviour – the importance of sequential files becomes obvious.

- *Random access files*, where any single component may be accessed at random, similar to an array access. The access to the components is usually done via some form of keys, which are associated with the component's location. Key and location together form the so-called index, which is a part of the file and must be managed by appropriate features of the operating system. But it should not be forgotten that this is just an organization superimposing the probably sequential structure of a secondary storage medium.

- *Indexed sequential files*, where random and sequential access is combined, i.e. a certain component may be accessed at random, and the next access (or read operation) retrieves the sequentially next component. Thus, indexed sequential files form a compromise between sequential and random access files.

3.5   Abstract Data Types

In the previous section we have seen that various possibilities exist to define structured data types to express real world problems. But we know that complex real world problems do not require only an abstraction in terms of data structures but also in terms of operations on data objects of such structured types. This means, that programming languages should provide constructs for the definition of *abstract data types*.

The fundamental ideas are that data and the appropriate operations on it belong together, and that implementation details are hidden to those who use the abstract data types (i.e. the concept of information hiding as described by Parnas [PARN 72]). Thus, the features which must be provided by programming languages to allow the definition of abstract data types can be summarized as follows:

- Features to *declare* new types.

- Features to *name* new types.

- Features to *specify* operations to manipulate data objects of these new types.

- Features to *hide* implementation details about both the objects and the operations.

The concept that data and the appropriate operations on it should form a syntactic unit (i.e. the concept of abstract data types) was initially introduced with SIMULA 67 and its *class* construct. Other languages followed, such as MODULA-2 and OBERON with the *module* construct, ADA with the *package* construct, or CLU [LISK 81] with the *cluster* construct.

As an example for an abstract data type we show how a queue and operations on it can be promulgated using MODULA-2, which distinguishes between *definition modules* – acting as user interfaces representing types and operations – and the *implementation modules* hiding all details about types and operations. A possible MODULA-2 definition module could then be:

```
DEFINITION MODULE QueueHandler;

    TYPE    Queue;      (* FIFO type of a queue *)
            Element;    (* an element of a queue *)

    PROCEDURE Empty (q: Queue): BOOLEAN;
    (* TRUE if q contains no elements *)

    PROCEDURE Insert (VAR q: Queue; e: Element);
    (* e becomes the last element in q *)

    PROCEDURE Get (q: Queue;  VAR e: Element);
    (* if q not empty, e becomes the first element *)
    (* of q, the first element in q is deleted *)
```

```
PROCEDURE Delete (VAR q: Queue; e: Element);
(* if e is in q, e is deleted *)

PROCEDURE Length (q: Queue): CARDINAL;
(* length of q *)
```

```
END QueueHandler.
```

Now, programmers who want to use the abstract data type import the type and operations from the given user interface, i.e. the definition module. They do not need to know anything about the implementation. The example shows, that MODULA-2 allows the declaration of so-called opaque types by which it is possible to hide the type's implementation.

The shown concept is the same as for elementary data types. For instance, considering a data object of type real. We are interested in the usage of such a data object and not in its implementation, i.e. we clearly distinguish between usage and implementation. This differentiation allows the user to consider an object in an abstract way, no matter whether it is based on an elementary data type or an abstract data type as introduced above.

3.6   Type Checking

We all know that, for example, the multiplication of a boolean with a real data object makes no sense. Inconsistencies of that kind can be recognized by certain type checking mechanisms. *Type checking* is the practice of ensuring that data objects which are somehow related are of compatible types. Two objects are related

- by forming the left and right side of an operator;

- by forming the left and right side of an assignment statement;

- by being actual and formal parameters.

Consistency checks which are made before the execution of a source program (i.e. by the compiler) are said to be *static checks*, while those checks performed during the execution of a source program are called *dynamic checks* (or *run-time checks*). Checking the syntax is an example for static checks, while *type checks* are an example of checks which often can be done statically, and which sometimes must be done dynamically.

For example, considering the following declaration

```
str :   ARRAY [0..80] OF CHAR;
i   :   INTEGER;
```

Then, in general, it cannot be guaranteed statically that the condition $0 \leq i \leq 80$ is fulfilled when using `str[i]`, i.e. this check has to be done dynamically. But, for example, it can be checked statically, whether the assignment

```
str[i] := ch;
```

is allowed, i.e. whether both sides of the assignment statement are of compatible types. Static type checking is usually supported by so-called symbol tables (see [TEUF 89], for example).

Obviously, the reliability of a certain programming language depends strongly on the provided type checking. If – like in separately compiled FORTRAN 77 subroutines – the type of actual and formal parameters can differ, it is clear that serious problems can occur during the program execution.

It is desirable to do as many static type checking as possible, since dynamic type checking can become very expensive. The reason for this is, that the compiler has to provide structures to hold information about certain data objects, and to generate additional code to perform dynamic type checking. The way how type checking is performed for a certain programming language goes along with the concept of type binding (cf Chapter 3.2) for this language.

3.7   Implementation of Data Types

For the implementation of data types we have to consider, how data objects of a particular type can be represented on the computer, and how the appropriate operations can be realized.

Elementary Data Types

The storage representation of integer and real types is usually supported by the hardware, i.e. the number representation of the computer system is used to represent fixed-point and floating-point numbers. If the target machine wouldn't provide, for example, a floating-point representation of numbers, the representation had to be simulated by software, what, obviously, becomes more expensive. The arithmetic operations also directly correspond to the fixed-point and floating-point arithmetic of the computer.

ALGOL 60 represents booleans as literals, while languages like PASCAL or ADA represent data objects of type boolean as an enumeration type, which can be mapped onto integer values. Since a byte is often the smallest addressable unit on a computer, not a single bit, but a byte is used to store boolean data objects. The interpretation could be, if one bit is 0, the data object is said to be *false* and it is *true* if all bits are 1. Logical operators are usually supported by the hardware.

The representation of data objects of type character are most often supported by the operating system and/or hardware. Normally we find a representation which is based on some standard character sets.

Structured Data Types

In general, storage representation of structured data types is not more complicated than the representation of elementary data types. The difference between elementary and structured data types is that structured types are an aggregation of elementary or user-defined (structured) types. The principal idea for implementing structured data types is a *descriptor* followed by the components of the type. The descriptor contains information about the aggregation of the structure and possibly also some run-time information; it gains its full meaning with dynamic structures.

For example, the two-dimensional array a[3..4, 2..5] of Figure 3.4 could be implemented by an descriptor followed by the array elements in adjacent memory locations as shown in Figure 3.7. Now, in this representation the base address (base$_a$) is the address of the memory location containing the number of dimensions.

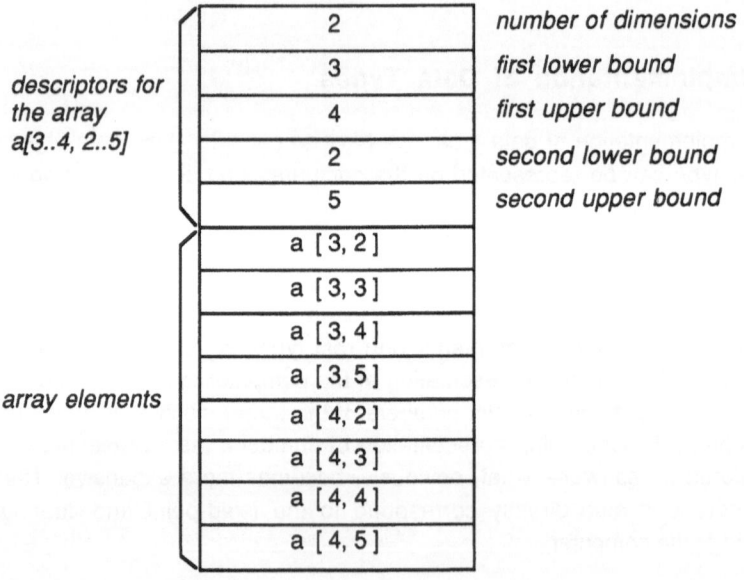

Fig. 3.7. Possible representation of the array a[3..4, 2..5] using row-major form

Analogically, the descriptor of a record type could contain the number of fields, information about the fields (e.g. upper and lower array bounds), and so on.

For recursively defined data structures (dynamic data structures) it is necessary to allocate storage during program execution. This is usually done by allocating the required storage from the *heap*, which is a storage pool from which space can be allocated and freed at any time and in any order during the execution of a program. Usually space is allocated on the stack for a pointer, which points to a storage block in the heap containing the data and a descriptor indicating the size of the data object etc. The situation is illustrated in Figure 3.8.

In general, heap allocation is not very complicated, but a requirement is the availability of a heap management. Since it is possible to deallocate storage in any order, strategies to manage and to combine the free storage blocks are necessary. Free storage blocks are usually linked together in a free-list (cf Figure 3.8).

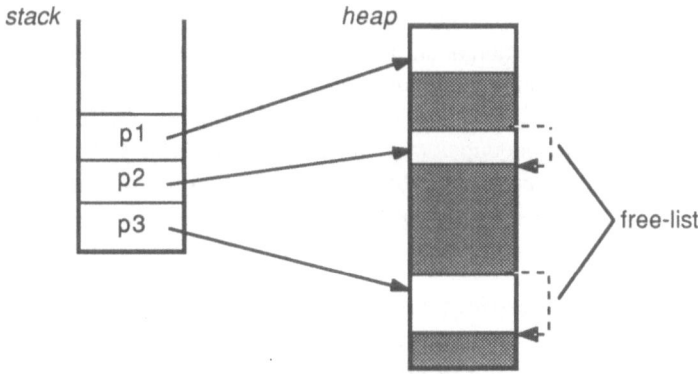

Fig. 3.8. Heap allocation

With the *dispose* procedure in PASCAL or MODULA-2 storage can explicitly be deallocated, and in such languages it is normally the user's responsibility to free storage. But other languages require implicit deallocation or garbage collection (i.e. the process to find unused space in the heap and to return it to the free-list). There are different strategies available for implicit deallocation. The simplest way to deallocate implicitly is to use *reference counts*, i.e. a counter indicating the number of pointers that exist to the data object. A zero counter causes that the storage space of the data object is inserted into the free-list.

3.8   Variables: Scope and Lifetime

We already introduced abstraction as a basic concept in programming and in the usage of programming languages. Now, one of the simplest kinds of abstraction is a variable. A *variable* simply can be seen as an abstraction of a cluster of memory locations representing one or more physical memory cells. Variables are bound to certain attributes:

- name and address,

- type and value,

- lifetime and scope.

Programming languages usually allow the definition of a variable's name as an alphanumeric string starting with a letter. Several languages, such as FORTRAN, restrict the length of a name, others like MODULA-2 do not (but it should be noted that sometimes an implementation dependent length restriction can be found, particularly for PASCAL implementations). Blanks are normally not allowed within a variable's name (an exception is ALGOL 60), and upper and lower case letters are distinguished in some languages (e.g. in ALGOL 60 or MODULA-2), while in others they are not distinguished (e.g. in PASCAL or FORTRAN). A variable is bound to a certain memory location via the appropriate address of the location and a reference to that location within a program is achieved by using a variable's name.

The type of a variable specifies the range of values which can be associated with that variable, and it specifies the set of operations which can be applied to manipulate variables of that type. For example, the values of variables of type boolean can be *true* or *false* and the allowed operations on such variables are given by the logical operators of a programming language. The binding of a value to a variable is dynamic, since the value can be changed during program execution by assignment of new values. In contrast to this, *constants* can be seen as static variables not allowing their value to be changed during program execution.

The discussion about scope and lifetime of a variable became important especially in block-oriented programming languages. The *scope* of a variable is described by the range of statements within the program over which the variable can be manipulated and accessed by its name. The *lifetime* of a variable is described by that part of the program's execution time in which the variable is bound to a memory location. Considerations about both, scope and lifetime, are substantial, since they determine the way in which a variable (or also other entities of a program) can have effects. By effects we mean, for example, the manipulation and accessibility of a memory location using a variable's name.

The difference between scope and lifetime of a variable can easily be exemplified considering, for example, a SIMULA 67 program consisting of several blocks. A block in SIMULA 67 (similar to ALGOL 60) is a unit consisting of declarations and a succeeding set of statements which together are treated as one statement. Therefore, those declarations and statements are labeled by a *begin-end* pair. In SIMULA 67 a block may be introduced at each point of a program where a single statement is allowed. An example for such a program is given in Figure 3.9, while the appropriate scopes and lifetimes of the variables are given in Figure 3.10.

```
BEGIN
        REAL   X, Y;
        INTEGER   I, J, K;

        statements block 1.1

        BEGIN
              REAL   X1;
              INTEGER   A, J;

              statements block 2.1

              BEGIN
                    REAL   X;
                    INTEGER   A, K;

                    statements block 3.1

              END;

              statements block 2.1

              BEGIN
                    REAL   A, B;
                    INTEGER   H, I;

                    statements block 3.2

              END;

              statements block 2.1

        END;

        statements block 1.1

END;
```

Fig. 3.9. A SIMULA 67 program shell containing several blocks

The variables which are declared in a certain block are said to be local to this block. Figure 3.10 shows that the lifetime of the variables of a block correspond to the blocks lifetime. It can also be seen how scope and lifetime of a variable of a block differ. For example, variable J of block 1.1 is bound to a memory location during the whole lifetime of block 1.1, while it is not known in the inner blocks, i.e. block 2.1, block 3.1, and block 3.2, since there is another variable declared with the same name in block 2.1.

		Block 1.1					Block 2.1			Block 3.1			Block 3.2			
		X	Y	I	J	K	X1	A	J	X	A	K	A	B	H	I
B1.1		sl	sl	sl	sl	sl										
		sl	sl	sl	sl	sl										
	B2.1	sl	sl	sl	l	sl	sl	sl	sl							
		sl	sl	sl	l	sl	sl	sl	sl							
		B3.1	l	sl	sl	l	l	sl	l	sl	sl	sl	sl				
		l	sl	sl	l	l	sl	l	sl	sl	sl	sl				
		sl	sl	sl	l	sl	sl	sl	sl							
		B3.2	sl	sl	l	l	sl	sl	l	sl				sl	sl	sl	sl
		sl	sl	l	l	sl	sl	l	sl				sl	sl	sl	sl
		sl	sl	sl	l	sl	sl	sl	sl							
		sl	sl	sl	sl	sl										

Fig. 3.10.   Scopes (s) and lifetimes (l) of the variables of Figure 3.9

4 Expressions and Control Structures

Sense and purpose of programs is the manipulation of some data represented by variables. In general, manipulation cannot simply be done by the assignment of certain values, but by the evaluation of expressions and the assignment of the evaluation's result to variables. Thus, *expressions* specify how values have to be calculated, i.e. they describe rules for elaborating a value. The elements of expressions are operands (may be function calls) which are combined by operators.

Beside the concept of abstraction we find in programming languages another very important concept. This is the concept of control mechanisms. *Control structures* allow the programmer to define the order of execution of statements. The availability of mechanisms that allow such a control makes programming languages powerful in their usage for the solution of complex problems. Usually problems cannot be solved just by sequencing some expressions or statements, rather they require in certain situations

- decisions – depending on some conditions – about which of some alternatives has to be executed, and/or

- to repeat or iterate parts of a program an arbitrary times – probably also depending on some conditions.

Imperative programming languages provide several control constructs to support selective or repetitive execution.

The subject of this Chapter is to introduce expressions and operators, in which we can also find some (implicit) control mechanisms. This introduction is followed by a discussion of control structures on statement level, as well as on the level of program units.

4.1   Expressions and Operators

According to Wirth expressions can be defined informally as follows [WIRT 76]: "*An expression consists of a term, followed by an operator, followed by a term. (The two terms constitute the operands of the operator.) A term is either a variable – represented by an identifier – or an expression enclosed in parentheses.*" This definition is slightly inexact, since it considers only binary operators. On the other hand, this definition shows that our above given definition is incomplete in the sense that parentheses and most of all recursion are not mentioned. In fact, expressions represent the simplest examples of recursively definable objects.

The most important question in the evaluation of expressions is in which *order* the evaluation is done. For example, if we consider the arithmetic expression

        X + Y * Z - 1

it is from a pure mathematical point of view clear what the result must be. Assuming X, Y, and Z to be 1, 2, and 4, respectively, the result of the expression is 8, because we first multiplied Y by Z and then added X and subtracted 1. We implicitly followed some priority rules for mathematical operations. We can get totally different results, if we do not have such priority rules. Other results of the given arithmetic expression could be 7, 9, or 11, depending on the order of evaluation.

To be sure that each implementation of a programming language uses the same order of evaluation and that (arithmetic or logical) operators are used in a common sense (i.e. according to mathematical definitions), programming languages introduce priorities for operators. Then, the rule is that the higher the priority of an operator within an expression the sooner the operation is performed. Operations of the same priority are typically evaluated left to right (an obvious exception is the exponentation operator), while parentheses are used to define other orders of evaluation. In FORTRAN, for example, we find the following priority ranking of operations (in decreasing order):

- exponentation,
- multiplication and division,
- addition and subtraction,
- relational operators,
- negation,
- logical and,
- logical or.

Other languages may use slightly different priority rules. A comparison of the precedence of operators in the languages FORTRAN, ALGOL 60, PL/1, PASCAL and ADA can be found in [HORO 84].

Boolean expressions differ from arithmetic expressions in that way that the result of a boolean expression can probably already be determined by knowing the value of one operand. For example, the boolean expression

    A OR (B AND C)

is always true whenever A is true. This means, that the subexpression

    (B AND C)

must not be evaluated if A is already true. A similar situation can be found if the two logical operators are exchanged:

    A AND (B OR C)

This expression is always false whenever A is false, i.e. the subexpression

    (B OR C)

must not be evaluated if A is already false.

Compiler writers sometimes use such a knowledge in the implementation of the evaluation of both arithmetic and boolean expressions. Unfortunately, this can cause inconsistencies and incompatibilities. For example, considering the expression

    (X <> 0.0) AND (Y/X <= 1.0)

it is clear that the rightmost subexpression must not be evaluated if X = 0.0. So, if a compiler produces code which already determines the result of the expression to be false in this case, no problems will occur with Y/X. But when we compile the program with a compiler that always produces code which evaluates the whole expression, we will run into a divide-by-zero error when the leftmost subexpression is false (i.e. X = 0.0). To overcome such problems we find, for instance, in ADA the possibility to define explicitly so-called *short-circuit evaluations* of boolean expressions using the operators

        and then   **and**   or else

where the left hand operand is always evaluated first and the right hand operand is only evaluated if it is necessary in order to determine the result. In MODULA-2 we find only short-circuit evaluations, while the evaluation of boolean expressions in PASCAL is implementation dependent.

4.2   Implicit and Explicit Control

Control structures in programming languages can be distinguished to be *implicit* or *explicit*. An implicit control structure in a programming language is the default of execution of statements or expressions. For example, the above discussed priority of operators is such an implicit control structure, which can be changed explicitly by the programmer using parentheses. Another example of implicit control is given by an implicit call of an exception handling routine.

Explicit control structures allow the programmer to replace the implicit, i.e. default, control structure of a programming language. Sequential machines have the implicit control structure that in a sequence of statements, one after another is executed. Now, programming languages provide, for example, selection and repetition statements to modify explicitly the default sequence of execution, or procedure call mechanisms to allow the programmer to define the control flow between program units.

4.3   Selection Statements

As we already mentioned, certain situations in the solution of a problem may require a decision (dependent on a certain input) about which of some alternatives has to be executed. Selection or conditional statements like

- the IF statement, and

- the CASE statement

allow a programmer to code such decisions.

The IF statement was already introduced in the early FORTRAN versions, but only in a very simple form:

```
IF  (C)  L1, L2, L3
```

where C represents the (arithmetic) condition and L1, L2, and L3 are labels. The semantics of this statement is that we branch to the statement with the label L1, L2, or L3 depending on whether the result of the evaluation of condition C is negative, zero, or positive, respectively.

Today we find in programming languages the form of IF statements as introduced by ALGOL 60:

```
IF  expression  THEN  statements 1  ELSE  statements 2
```

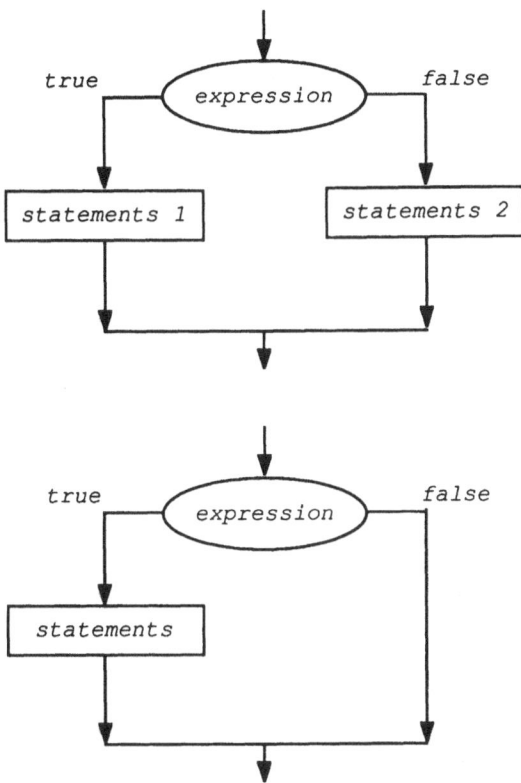

Fig. 4.1. Structure of IF statements

where the ELSE clause of the statement must not necessarily exist. Figure 4.1 represents this structure diagrammatically. The semantics of such an IF statement is that the alternative described by *statements 1* is executed if the value of *expression* is true, otherwise the alternative described by *statements 2* is executed. For example,

        IF   X <> 0.0   THEN   X := Y/X   ELSE   X := X + 1.0

means that if X = 0.0 we increment X by 1 and in all other cases we assign the value Y/X to X.

Clearly, *statements 1* can again be a conditional statement, which then can lead to the following well-known ambiguity problem:

        IF   E1   THEN   IF   E2   THEN   S1   ELSE   S2

Now, it is not clear whether the statements S2 of the ELSE clause belong to the IF statement with the condition E2 or to the IF statement with the condition E1. The ambiguity can be shown by considering the following grammar, which allows the generation of two different parse trees (cf Figure 4.2) for the above given IF statement:

stmt → IF *expr* THEN *stmt* | IF *expr* THEN *stmt* ELSE *stmt* | *other* .

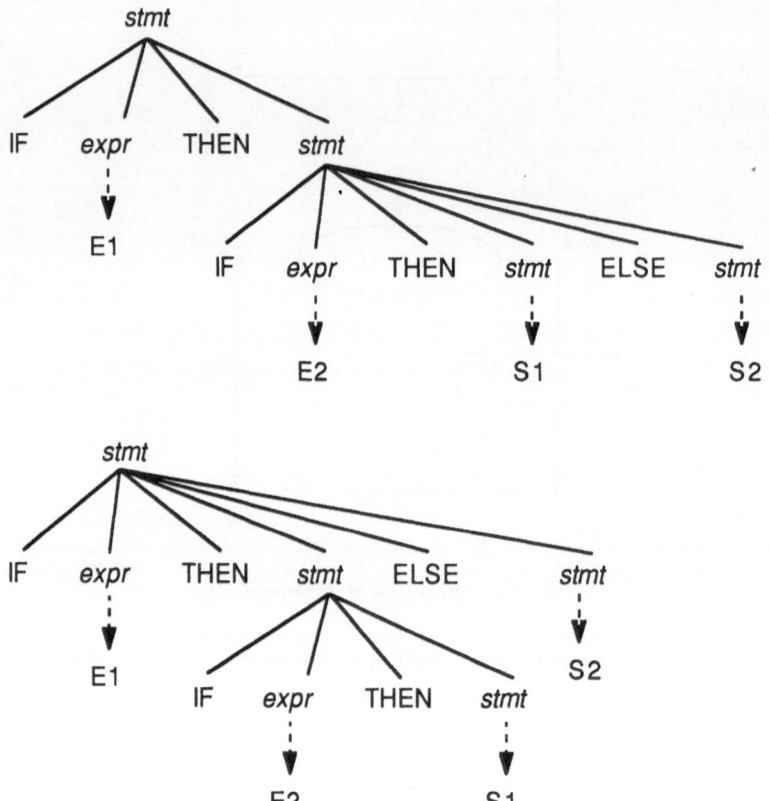

Fig. 4.2. Different parse trees for IF E1 THEN IF E2 THEN S1 ELSE S2

Programming languages like PASCAL usually interpret such IF statements in the way of the upper parse tree, i.e. each ELSE clause is matched with the most recent IF statement. ALGOL 60 avoids such ambiguities by not allowing conditional statements following a THEN, i.e. BEGIN-END brackets must be used to express the meaning of the upper parse tree:

```
IF   E1   THEN   BEGIN   IF   E2   THEN   S1   ELSE   S2   END
```

In MODULA-2 every control structure (and, therefore, also the IF statement) has an explicit termination, which is usually an END. Thus, in MODULA-2 the above given ambiguity problem does not occur, because with the placement of the END's it is clear which IF statement goes with which ELSE clause:

```
IF   E1   THEN   IF   E2   THEN   S1   ELSE   S2   END   END
```

Similar approaches can be found in ALGOL 68, where IF statements are terminated with a FI, or in ADA, where the termination of an IF statement is an END IF.

For nested IF statements of the form

```
IF   E1   THEN   S1
ELSE IF   E2   THEN   S2
        ELSE IF   E3   THEN   S3
            ...   ...   ...

            ...   ...   ...
                ELSE IF   Ek   THEN   Sk
                    ELSE
                            S(k+1)
                    END
                END
            END
        END
END
```

we usually find some form of an ELSIF construct, which avoids the writing of all of the END's:

```
IF   E1   THEN   S1
ELSIF   E2   THEN   S2
ELSIF   E3   THEN   S3
...   ...   ...
ELSIF   Ek   THEN   Sk
ELSE   S(k+1)
END
```

Such a structure represents a selection out of (k+1) alternatives. Programming languages like ADA, PASCAL, or MODULA-2 provide for such multi-way decisions the CASE statement. Here, the result of the evaluation of an expression determines the actual selection. For example, the MODULA-2 syntax for CASE statements is as follows:

```
CASE   expression  OF
    CaseLabelList1 :   S1
|   CaseLabelList2 :   S2
|   CaseLabelList3 :   S3
    ... ... ...
|   CaseLabelListk :   Sk
ELSE      S(k+1)
END
```

The *expression* has the function of a selector and *CaseLabelList* may be a single constant or a list of constants of the same type as the expression's result, which must be an ordinal type in MODULA-2. The structure of the CASE statement is diagrammatically shown in Figure 4.3.

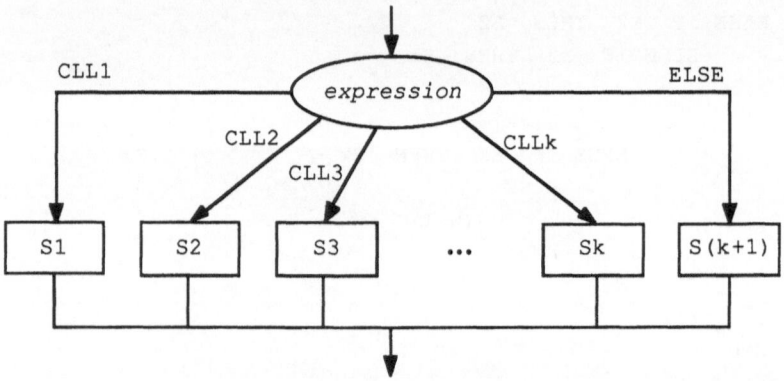

Fig. 4.3   Structure of CASE statements

Other languages may provide a slightly different syntax for CASE statements. For example, not every PASCAL implementation provides an ELSE clause in a CASE statement and, if it is provided, it is usually called OTHERWISE. In ALGOL 68 the expression is of type integer, while ADA names the ELSE clause OTHERS and uses WHEN for the "|" in MODULA-2. In C the CASE statements are called SWITCH statements, the expression is of type integer, the term CASE is used like WHEN or "|", and the ELSE clause is called DEFAULT.

4.4   Repetition Statements

The requirement for repeating several statements within a program is a quite often occurring situation. A very simple example, which can be found in most programs, is the initialization of an array variable. Repetition statements like

- FOR statements

- WHILE, REPEAT, or LOOP statements

allow a programmer to code such repetitions. These two groups of repetition statements are commonly distinguished as counter-decided and condition-decided, respectively.

Again, already in the early FORTRAN versions we can find a very simple form of a counter-decided repetition (although it does not contain the keyword FOR), e.g.

```
      DO   111   I = 1,20
      X(I) = 0.0
111   CONTINUE
```

where 111 is a label with a CONTINUE statement terminating the repetition, I is the counter variable with the lower bound 1 and upper bound 20. All statements between the DO statement and the CONTINUE statement are repeated as many times as it is specified by the lower and upper bound for the counter variable.

In other programming languages, such as PASCAL, MODULA-2, or ADA, we find counter-decided repetitions based on the typical ALGOL-like FOR statement. One example is the following MODULA-2 syntax:

```
FOR cv := InitExpr TO FinExpr BY IncrExpr DO stmts END
```

where the BY clause must not necessarily exist. Fig 4.4 represents the principle structure of FOR statements diagrammatically. The semantics of such a FOR statement is as follows:

i.   The range of a counter (cv) is specified by an initial expression (InitExpr) and a final expression (FinExpr); if the counter value cv is an element of the specified range, continue with ii. otherwise continue with the statement following the FOR statement.

ii. Execute the statements (stmts) and continue with iii.

iii. If cv is greater or equal the value given by FinExpr, the repetition is stopped and it is continued with the statement following the FOR statement, otherwise (cv < FinExpr) cv is either incremented by 1 (which is the default) or it is incremented or decremented as specified by the BY clause (IncrExpr) and it is continued with ii.

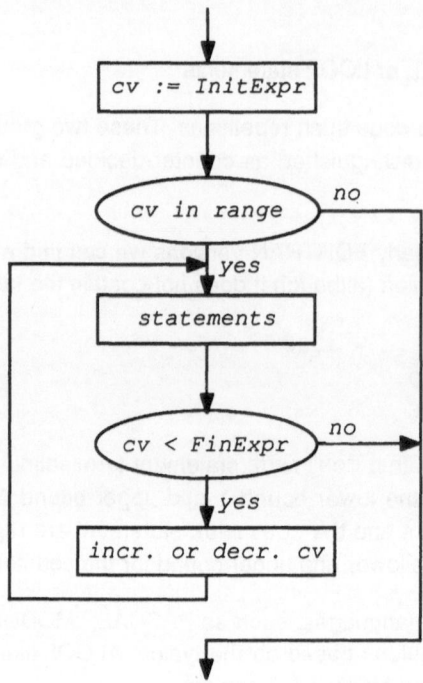

Fig. 4.4. Principle control flow for FOR statements

As usual different programming languages vary in the syntax for FOR statements, but there are also some differences in the semantics of FOR statements. The most important differences are

- whether the counter variable holds a defined value after the termination of the FOR statement,

- whether the counter variable is allowed to be changed by an assignment within the FOR statement,

- whether FinExpr and IncrExpr are evaluated only once, or each time the counter variable is checked against the final value and incremented/decremented.

In PASCAL and MODULA-2 the counter variable is undefined on exit from the FOR loop, while in ADA the counter variable only has the scope of the FOR statement and, thus, is not available outside. In ALGOL 60 the counter variable is only undefined if the FOR loop was normally terminated, and FinExpr and IncrExpr are re-evaluated each time they are needed. This is not done in languages like PASCAL or ADA.

Counter decided repetition can easily be applied in all those cases, where the number of repetitions is more or less known in advance (e.g. for some form of initialization). However, there are a lot of problems requiring an indefinite looping, i.e. the number of repetitions is not known in advance, but depends on some conditions (e.g. a search in a tree structure). For those cases condition-decided looping is provided.

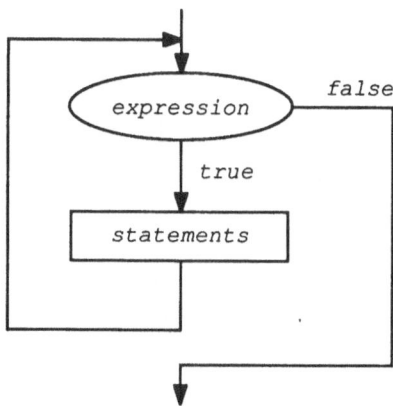

Fig. 4.5. Control flow for WHILE statements

The WHILE statement is the most common form of condition-decided looping. In general, we find a form as follows:

```
WHILE  expression  DO  statements  END
```

where the explicit termination of the statement is typical for MODULA-2 or ADA (using END LOOP). The flow of control for WHILE statements is shown in Figure 4.5. The semantics of WHILE statements is obvious. The condition is evaluated and the body of the WHILE statement is executed as long as the condition is true. Thus, the loop body may be entered zero or more times.

Similarly to the WHILE statement is the REPEAT statement as introduced by PASCAL. The major difference between these two condition-decided repetitions is that the loop body of REPEAT statements is executed at least once, i.e. the condition is evaluated not before, but after the execution of the loop body.

The MODULA-2 syntax for REPEAT statements is as follows:

```
REPEAT  statements  UNTIL  expression
```

We see that the REPEAT statement in MODULA-2 is not terminated with an END clause, but with the UNTIL clause. Figure 4.6 shows the appropriate flow of control diagrammatically.

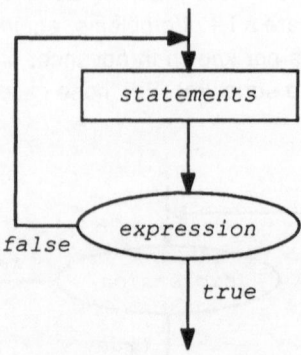

Fig. 4.6. Control flow for REPEAT statements

Additional to these two condition-decided repetition constructs we find in ADA and MODULA-2, for example, a LOOP statement providing infinite loops. Here it should be noted, that ADA uses the keyword LOOP for FOR and WHILE as well as for the actual infinite loops. This means, that ADA knows only the LOOP statement consisting of a *repetition specification* and the loop body. The repetition specification is used to define FOR or WHILE loops, or if it is omitted, to define infinite loops. The general form of a LOOP statement is (in MODULA-2 syntax)

```
LOOP    statements    END
```

The loop is terminated using the EXIT clause within `statements`, e.g.

```
IF    expression    THEN    EXIT    END
```

Obviously, it is possible to specify several conditions to exit from the loop. An infinite LOOP statement can replace both the REPEAT and the WHILE statement depending on when the condition will be tested for exiting the loop. Thus, the control flow of the LOOP statement as shown in Figure 4.7 can be understood as a combination of Figure 4.5 and Figure 4.6.

Obviously, we program a WHILE statement using the LOOP construct if the `expression` is evaluated first in the loop body, i.e. `statements 1` is the empty set. A REPEAT statement is represented if the `expression` evaluation is the last statement of the loop body, i.e. `statements 2` is the empty set. This implies that REPEAT and WHILE constructs (or even FOR constructs) are redundant in languages providing the LOOP construct. But the readability as well as the writability of programs is much greater, having several repetition statements available.

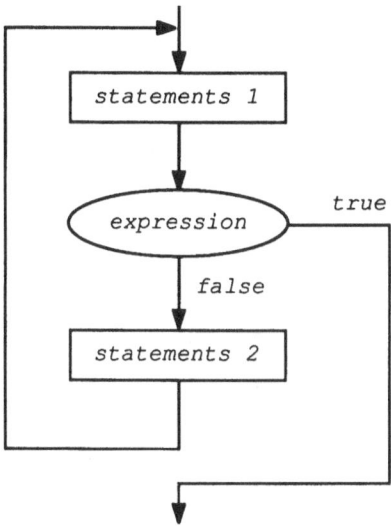

Fig. 4.7. Principle control flow for LOOP statements

4.5   Procedure Calls and Exception Handling

With the previous sections on expressions, selection statements, and repetition statements, we introduced several methods of control on expression and statement level. We already mentioned that there are certain mechanisms available allowing to direct the flow of control between parts or units of programs. Such mechanisms are

- procedures (simple or recursive ones),

- exception handling,

- coroutines, and

- tasks.

The simple PROCEDURE CALL allows the explicit, i.e. programmer defined flow control between statement sequences (or parts of a program), which is diagrammatically shown in Figure 4.8. The definition of a procedure assigns a name to a sequence of statements. This statement sequence can be executed using the language's call mechanism together with the defined name. In FORTRAN, for example, the execution of subroutines can be controlled using the CALL statement and the procedures name:

    CALL *subroutine name*   ,

while in PASCAL, MODULA-2, or ADA a procedure is invoked using just the procedure's name. Along with the CALL mechanism we find an inverse one, the RETRUN mechanism, by which the change of control back to the calling instance is specified. This mechanism can be either implicit (i.e. after the execution of the last statement of a procedure) or it can be explicit (i.e. it might be possible to terminate the execution of a procedure at any point in the procedure's body, by means of an explicit RETURN statement).

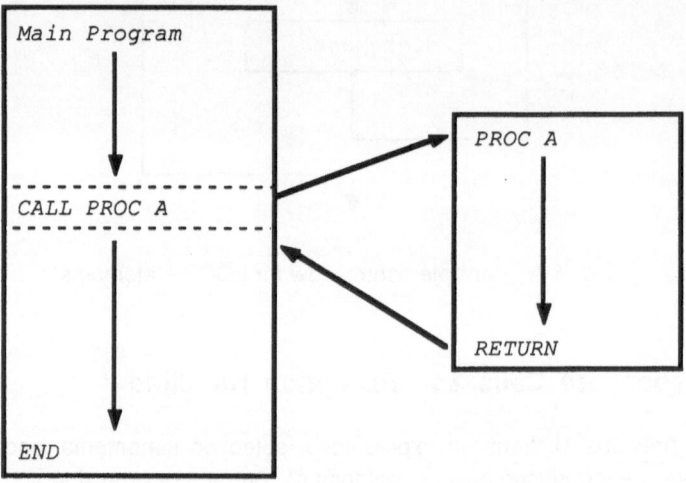

Fig. 4.8.   Procedure CALL-RETURN mechanism

The communication between several program units represented by the procedures and some form of a main program is usually done by *parameters*, which allow the exchange of data or information in general. Various parameter passing methods exist. They are described in Chapter 5.

Another – even if a little risky – way to communicate between program units is based on *side effects*. This means, that global variables are used for the communication, which can be changed within a procedure and thus form *implicit results* [PRAT 84] of the procedure. A clearly defined parameter list represents the specification of an interface between several program units and, therefore, describes exactly the effects on in/out parameters, i.e. the effects to the world outside the procedure. Obviously, the more we use non-local variables for an information exchange between program units, the harder it is to read and to understand a program and

the greater is the probability that unintentional situations occur, because it is difficult to overlook the range of effects.

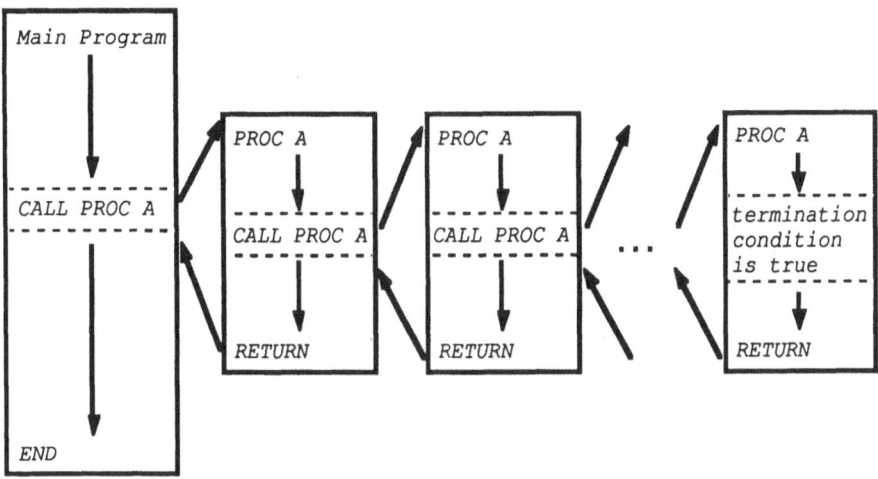

Fig. 4.9. Control flow for recursive procedures

One of the most powerful concepts of control in programming is that of *recursion*,
both for data control and sequence control. Recursion means, that an object (e.g. a
data structure or a procedure) is in some way specified in terms of itself. Considering procedures, we find recursion expressed in the way that a procedure A contains either a *direct* call of itself, or it contains an *indirect* call of itself via a procedure B, which is called by A and which, again, calls A. Obviously, to avoid infinite
loops of procedure calls, there must be a termination condition specified within the
procedure's body. The control flow for recursively called procedures is schemati-
cally shown in Figure 4.9. The concept of recursive procedure calls is provided by
all important programming languages.

While the behaviour of simple procedures is a static one in terms of memory allocation (in the simplest case a procedure call can just be replaced by the procedure's body), this is not true for recursive procedures. They are dynamic (i.e. it cannot be determined at compile time how often a procedure calls itself) and, thus,
they require a more sophisticated way of implementation. This will be discussed in
Chapter 5.

While procedure calls are an explicit control mechanism, *exception handling* is an
implicit control mechanism. Exception handling means that certain situations, such
as a divide-by-zero or an unexpected end-of-file, which can occur during the execution of a program, need some special processing. A number of programming languages provide exception handling features, among them are PL/1, CLU, or ADA.

An *exception handler* is nothing else but a subprogram or procedure which deals with the exception. These exceptions may occur

- by hardware interrupts (e.g. arithmetic overflow),

- by the operating system (e.g. end-of-file conditions),

- by checking code inserted by the compiler (e.g. subscript range errors),

- by checking code inserted by the programmer (e.g. using an explicit *raise* statement (ADA) in certain situations).

The concept of controlling the flow of control in the case of an exception is quite diverse in different languages. On the one hand, there are languages, like ADA, where we find the concept that, for instance, a procedure cannot resume from an exception, i.e. the program part where the exception occurred is simply terminated after the exception handler terminated. On the other hand, we find the concept, followed in languages like PL/1, that control is returned to where the exception occurred, i.e. some kind of repair can be done by the exception handler, and the program part where the exception occurred can be resumed. The latter is usually harder to understand for a programmer.

4.6   Coroutines and Tasks

The idea of procedures or subprograms is that we transfer control from one part of a program to another part (i.e. to a procedure) using the procedure call mechanism, and that – based on the return mechanism – control is transferred back to the calling instance after all statements of the procedure have been executed. Invoking a procedure causes the allocation of storage for local data structures, which is deallocated with the return to the calling instance.

Now, there are situations conceivable, where the body of a called procedure is only partly executed when control is transferred back to the calling instance and that the execution of the rest of the procedure's statements is suspended for a certain time. For example, the simulation of a *single server system* consisting of a *queue* and the *server*. Both, the queue and the server are mapped onto a procedure, where the queue-procedure simulates the arrival process of customers (e.g. a Poisson arrival stream), and the server-procedure simulates the service process (e.g. a negative exponential distribution of the service time). Obviously, this is a real life problem with two parallel cooperating processes, which on a sequential computer must be simulated in a quasi-parallel way, i.e. only one of the processes can be in execution at a time and control must be swapped between them. *Coroutines* provide a *synchronization* for such parallel cooperating processes.

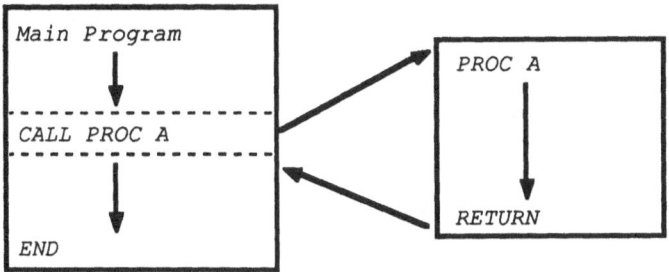

a) asymmetric flow of control

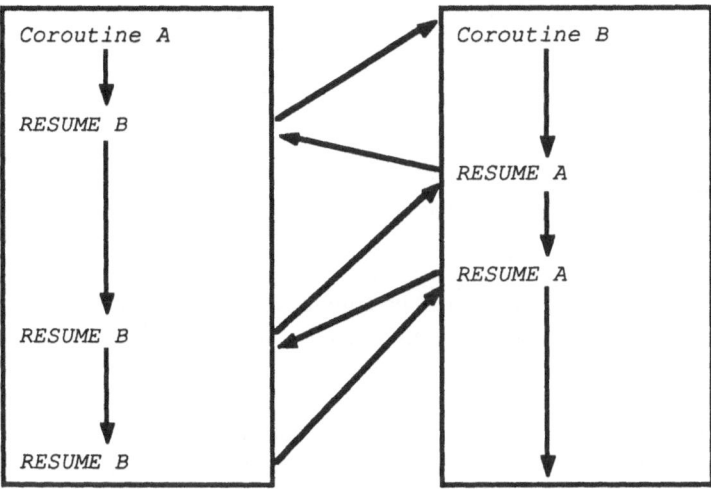

b) symmetric flow of control

Fig. 4.10.   Procedure and coroutine invocation

Coroutines are a form of procedures allowing the mutual activation of each other in an explicit way. As already mentioned, if control is transferred to a coroutine it executes only partially, and suspends a part of the execution for a certain time. Important is, that a coroutine resumes at that point where it last terminated when control is transferred to it and, therefore, that coroutines have several entry points. This is exactly the basic requirement for interleaved processes, such as in the above given example. While the flow of control for procedure calls is asymmetric, it is *symmetric* for the activation of coroutines. This is shown in Figure 4.10, where it is assumed that the transfer of control can be done using a RESUME statement. Procedures and coroutines are compared in Table 4.1.

Table 4.1.   Procedures and coroutines

Procedures	Coroutines
• transfer control	• transfer control
• execute (more or less) all statements	• execute only a part of the statements
• transfer control back to the calling instance	• suspend the execution of the rest of the statements and transfers control by activating another coroutine
• each activation is independent and execution starts with the first statement	• each activation continues with that statement following the statement which was executed last
• includes memory allocation, deallocation for local variables etc.	• no memory deallocation
• asymmetric flow of control	• symmetric flow of control

The most popular language containing coroutine features is SIMULA 67, but there are a few others, such as BLISS, for example, which provide also coroutine features. The language definition of MODULA-2 provides no features for symmetric control flow, but Wirth proposes with his SYSTEM module [WIRT 88a] sufficient features for coroutines: PROCESS, NEWPROCESS, TRANSFER. Most MODULA systems provide these features. Good examples how to use these features can be found in [GUTK 84], for example.

Any program unit that can be in concurrent execution with other program units is called a *task* (note: concurrent execution means not necessarily parallel execution on parallel hardware, rather a parallelism on an abstract logical level is meant, which then can also be performed on a single processor). While coroutines are used to describe interleaved processes with an explicit mutual activation, tasks are used to describe concurrent processes which can be considered to be more or less independent, i.e. they perform their activities independently to satisfy a common goal. Various examples can be found considering producer-consumer problems in operating systems, where one task produces certain entities and another one consumes these entities. Such examples show that features must be provided to control communication and interaction between tasks, features allowing the synchronization of tasks. Several synchronization mechanisms have been developed, among them are

- *semaphores,*

- *monitors,*

- *message-passing,* or *rendezvous.*

Semaphores were introduced by Dijkstra [DIJK 68a], [DIJK 68b] and were used, for example, in ALGOL 68, while Brinch Hansen introduced monitors with his CONCURRENT PASCAL [BRIN 75a]. The ideas of message-passing were introduced by Hoare [HOAR 78] and Brinch Hansen [BRIN 78] and applied in ADA to describe the synchronization of tasks. These mechanisms for the manipulation of the flow of control are described in more detail in Chapter 8.

5 Procedures

In the preceding Chapter we have already seen the importance of *subprograms* (or *procedures* and *functions*) as an instrument to manipulate the flow of control in a program system. Thus, in this Chapter we should talk about procedures in more detail. We have to discuss methods for parameter passing, overloading and generic concepts, as well as implementation techniques. But we want to start with a brief overview on the basic ideas behind procedures.

5.1   Basic Ideas

Procedures and functions (the difference between them will be discussed below) are program units which are syntactically separated and which are invoked by a special mechanism, the *procedure call*. Procedures or subprograms have already been introduced with the earliest programming languages, e.g. in assembly languages or in FORTRAN, but the intention of procedures has changed during the years. In the beginning procedures were a concept to shorten programs (i.e. the source code), and in doing so, to save memory. Statement sequences which were used on several points of a program were given a name and were separated and, therefore, covered the memory locations only once. This saves memory, but also increases the readability of complex programs (i.e. it is an approach towards structured programming). The abstraction concept was more or less inspired by the idea of reducing the size of the code (cf Figure 5.1a).

Today, procedures are still used to write multiply occurring code only once in a program, but the concept of abstraction in the usage of procedures has become more important, since procedures are now used to *modularize complex problems*. Procedures are a mechanism to control and reduce complexity of programming systems by grouping certain activities together into syntactically separated program units. Therefore, the multiple usage of program code is no longer a criterion for separating code, rather procedures represent more and more source code which is used only once within a program, but which performs some basic operations. This is shown in Figure 5.1b.

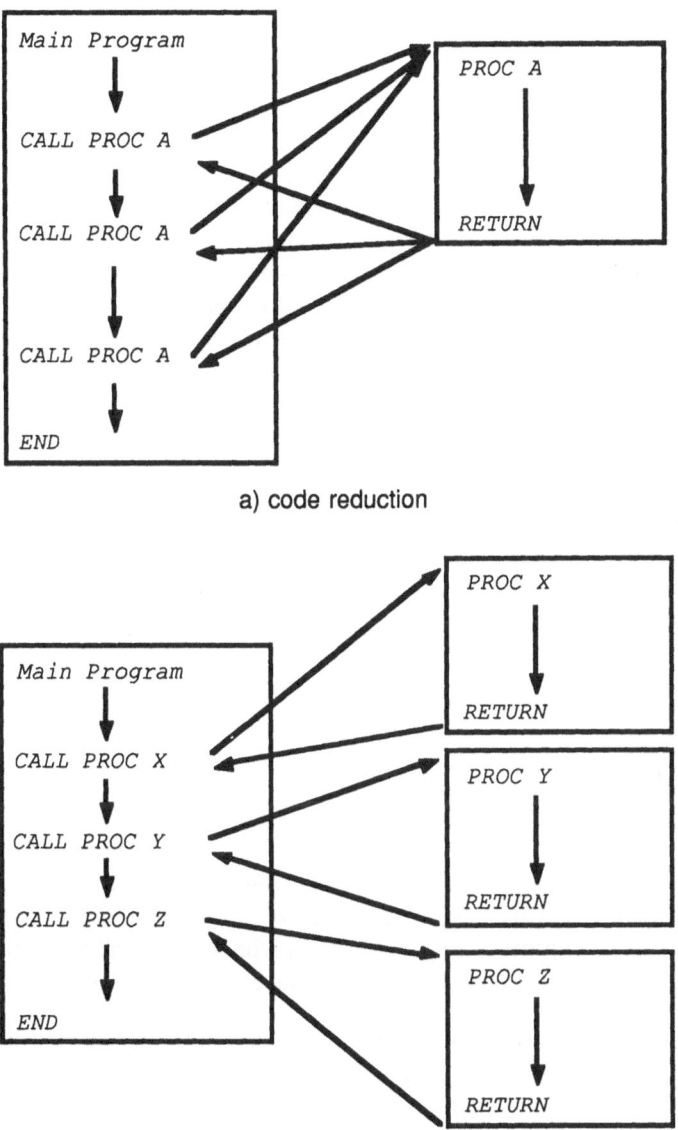

a) code reduction

b) complexity reduction

Fig. 5.1. Abstraction concepts using procedures

In the following, we introduce important terms and characteristics in the context of subprograms.

Procedures and Functions

Subprograms are often divided into procedures and functions. In general, the only difference between them is, that a function is a subprogram producing a result, i.e. it returns a value for the function name. Thus, a function is a form of an expression and, therefore, can be used wherever an expression can be used. In PASCAL we find for these two kinds of subprograms the keywords PROCEDURE and FUNCTION, while MODULA-2, for example, knows only PROCEDUREs, which can or cannot produce a result. In C, functions are the only available type of a subprogram. When we talk about procedures in the following, we mean also functions, unless we explicitly state a difference between them.

There are two concepts of returning a value from a function: In FORTRAN or PASCAL we assign the result value to the functions name and we terminate the function when the last statement is executed. In MODULA-2 or ADA we use an explicit RETURN-statement with the appropriate result value. This allows to have several exit points within a function. Most languages allow a function only to be of an elementary type, while, for example, ADA allows also the result to be a structured type, or LISP allows even the result to be a function itself.

Characteristics

Although procedures might be slightly different in their usage and implementation in different programming languages, there exist some common characteristics. Among them are:

- Procedures are referred to by a *name*. They usually have *local variable declarations*, as well as some *parameters* forming the communication interface to other procedures and the main program. In addition to this, functions are bound to a particular type, i.e. the type of the result they produce.

- A procedure has only *one entry point* (FORTRAN makes an exception, since it allows the execution of a subprogram to begin at any desired executable statement using the ENTRY statement; but the overall concept is the same as for single entry procedures).

- The procedure call mechanism *allocates* storage for local data structures.

- The procedure call mechanism *transfers control* to the called instance and *suspends* the calling instance during the execution of the procedure (i.e. no form of parallelism or concurrency is allowed).

- The procedure return mechanism *deallocates* storage for local data structures.

- The procedure return mechanism *transfers control back* to the calling instance when the procedure execution terminates.

The implementation of these characteristics is described later in this Chapter.

Structure and Specification

The typical structure of a subprogram is given by the following procedure specification (adopted from MODULA-2 syntax):

```
PROCEDURE name (parameter list);
     declarations
     BEGIN
          statements       (* procedure body *)
     END name;
```

Such a procedure definition bounds a name to a sequence of statements (and data declarations) and describes the actions standing behind the procedure abstraction. A subprogram is invoked with a procedure call statement, which is usually (e.g. in MODULA-2, PASCAL or ADA) just the name of the procedure.

5.2   Parameter Passing

As we have already seen, parameters are those features of a procedure which allow a controlled and well-defined communication, i.e. exchange of information or data, between the procedure and the outside world. In programming languages we distinguish between

- *formal parameters*, and

- *actual parameters*.

Formal parameters are part of the specification of a procedure, they are local data objects within a procedure. The specification of formal parameters describes the way of data exchange in terms of type and input/output. For example,

```
PROCEDURE COMP (a, b: INTEGER; VAR c: BOOLEAN);
```

describes (in MODULA-2 syntax) the two formal parameters a and b to be of type INTEGER, and to be only input parameters, while the formal parameter c is of type BOOLEAN and is an input/output parameter.

Actual parameters are those parameters which are actually used when the procedure is called, i.e. they are data objects which the calling and the called instance have in common. Obviously, they must correspond to the specification of the formal parameters.

The binding between actual and formal parameters is usually done by the position, i.e. the k-th actual parameter is bound to the k-th formal parameter. ADA allows also another way of calling subprograms, where it is possible to state explicitly the association between formal and actual parameters. For example, consider the following procedure declaration:

```
procedure P (P1: in INTEGER; P2: in out BOOLEAN);
```

A positional call could be given by

```
P (I, B);
```

while a call where the association between formal and actual parameters is explicitly stated could be given as

```
P (P2 => B, P1 => I);
```

The example shows that the actual parameters can be given in any order using the association method.

Several methods are known to pass parameters from a calling instance to a procedure. These methods differ in their effects and can roughly be classified as methods only for input, or methods for in/out parameters. The methods are explained using the following principle schema of a procedure declaration and call (Figure 5.2 to Figure 5.5).

```
VAR   a, b :   INTEGER;
      PROCEDURE   P (p1, p2: INTEGER);
      BEGIN
            ...
      END P;
      ...
      P (a, b);
```

Call by Value

Call by value means that the value of the actual parameter is copied into the storage space of the formal parameter, when calling the procedure (cf Figure 5.2). Thus, formal parameters can be treated like local variables, i.e. storage allocation and access is the same as for local variables. Code must be generated to perform the copy operation, which can result in a considerable overhead when passing large data structures by value. Clearly, that in this case data can be passed into a procedure, but not out from the procedure.

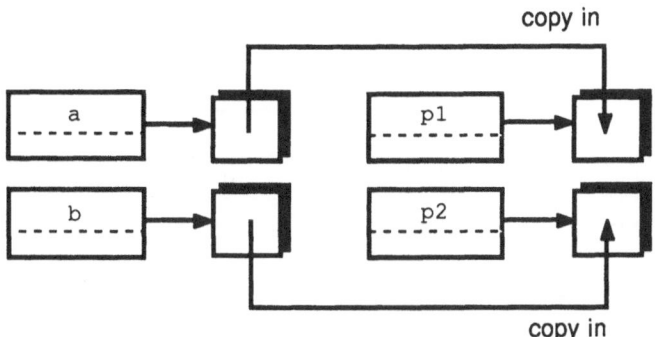

Fig. 5.2. Call by value

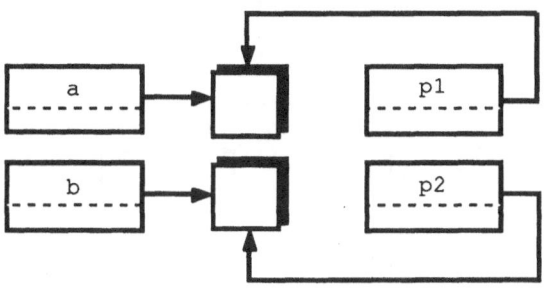

Fig. 5.3. Call by reference

Call by Reference

Call by reference means that the address of the actual parameter is passed to the procedure, instead of the value (cf Figure 5.3). Thus, the location of the formal parameter contains just the address where to find and/or to change the data. So, each parameter access requires instructions for indirect addressing. Intensive access to reference parameters in a procedure can therefore cause an overhead. Clearly, that in this case data can be passed into and out from a procedure.

Call by Value-result

Call by value-result is in-between call by reference and call by value. When entering the procedure, the actual parameter is copied to the formal parameter and it is copied back when terminating the procedure (cf Figure 5.4). Thus, parameters can be accessed like local variables. Since there are two copy operations, the disadvantage of the call by value technique is doubled, but the disadvantage of the call by reference technique does not occur. Obviously, this technique should only be applied when passing simple type variables.

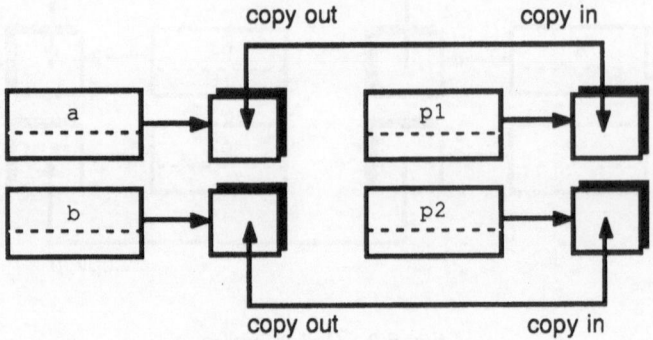

Fig. 5.4. Call by value-result

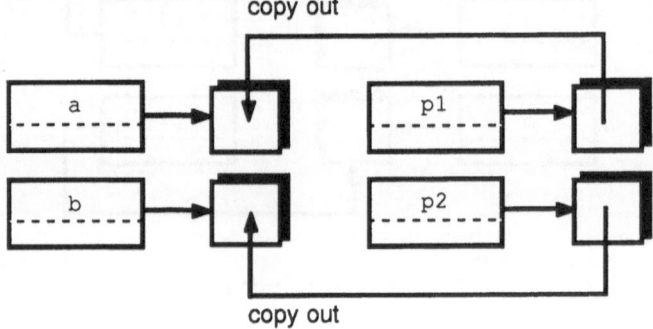

Fig. 5.5. Call by result

Call by Result

Call by result means that a value is assigned to the formal parameter during the procedure's execution. This value of the formal parameter is copied to the actual parameter on termination of the procedure (cf Figure 5.5). Thus, this method is similar to call by value-result, except that the actual parameter is not copied to the formal parameter on entering the procedure. Information or data can only be passed out from a procedure using call by result.

Call by Name

Call by name means that the actual parameter substitutes textually the formal parameter, whenever it occurs. The concept is more or less a historic one. It was introduced in ALGOL 60 and is not used in recent programming languages.

We quote from the report [NAUR 63]: "*Any formal parameter not quoted in the value list (i.e. call by value parameter) is replaced, throughout the procedure body, by the corresponding actual parameter, after enclosing this latter in parentheses wherever syntactically possible. Possible conflicts between identifiers inserted through this process and other identifiers already present within the procedure body will be avoided by suitable systematic changes of the formal or local identifiers involved.*"

The traditional technique of implementation is to treat the procedure as a macro, i.e. the compiler replaces each call of the procedure by the procedure's body. Possible conflicts between names of variables may rise with this substitution; they are avoided by renaming the local names and, thus, local names are kept distinct from names in the calling block. The principle is given in the following example:

```
procedure  P(k);
integer k;
begin
      integer i, x;
      i := i * n;    x := k - i;
end;
```

Now, assuming that we have a nonlocal variable i defined in the block where the above procedure is defined and called:

```
begin
      integer i;
      ...
      P (i);
      ...
end;
```

This will result in the following substitution:

```
begin
      integer i;
      ...
      j := j * n;    x := i - j;
      ...
end;
```

where the procedure call statement is replaced by the procedure body and the formal parameter is textually substituted by the actual parameter. The occurring naming conflict is solved by renaming the procedures local variable i to j.

Table 5.1 gives several examples on which passing techniques are used by which programming language.

Table 5.1.   Programming languages and parameter passing techniques

Passing Technique	Examples of Programming Languages
Call by Value	PASCAL, MODULA-2, SIMULA 67, ALGOL 60, C, ADA, PL/1 (if actual parameter is an expression)
Call by Reference	PASCAL, MODULA-2, SIMULA 67, FORTRAN (standard), PL/1 (standard), C (if actual parameter is an array)
Call by Value-result	ALGOL-W, ADA, FORTRAN
Call by Result	ADA
Call by Name	ALGOL 60

To conclude this section we compare the results of the different passing methods by considering the following program fragment:

```
...
var   k  :  integer;
      a  :  array [1..2] of integer;
...
procedure modeTest (mode x: integer);
begin
     a[1] := 10;
     k := 3;
     x := x * k;
     writeln('a[1]: ', a[1]);
     writeln('a[2]: ', a[2]);
     writeln('k   : ', k);
end;
...
```

```
begin
     a[1] := 1;
     a[2] := 2;
     k := 1;
     modeTest (a[k]);
     writeln('a[1]: ', a[1]);
     writeln('a[2]: ', a[2]);
     writeln('k    : ', k);
     modeTest (k);
     writeln('a[1]: ', a[1]);
     writeln('a[2]: ', a[2]);
     writeln('k    : ', k);
end;
```

where mode in the formal parameter list of a procedure indicates call by value, reference, value result, result, or name. Table 5.2 shows the output of the program for the first three of those parameter passing methods.

Table 5.2.   Differences in parameter passing

Output	Call by Value	Call by Reference	Call by Value Result
in 1st proc. call	a[1]: 10 a[2]: 2 k : 3	a[1]: 30 a[2]: 2 k : 3	a[1]: 10 a[2]: 2 k : 3
after 1st proc. call	a[1]: 10 a[2]: 2 k : 3	a[1]: 30 a[2]: 2 k : 3	a[1]: 3 a[2]: 2 k : 3
in 2nd proc. call	a[1]: 10 a[2]: 2 k : 3	a[1]: 10 a[2]: 2 k : 9	a[1]: 10 a[2]: 2 k : 3
after 2nd proc. call	a[1]: 10 a[2]: 2 k : 3	a[1]: 10 a[2]: 2 k : 9	a[1]: 10 a[2]: 2 k : 9

In the case of call by result, a syntax error should occur (considering an ADA-like environment) since the value of x in $x := x * k;$ is undefined.

Call by name is not included in the table, because it would result in a run-time error with the first procedure call, i.e. with

```
     k := 3;
```

the next statement

```
a[k] := a[k] * k;
```

results in an index range error.

5.3   Procedure Parameters

Several programming languages allow the passing of procedures or functions to subprograms. Such parameters are called *procedure parameters* or *formal procedures* (function parameters or formal functions). The usefulness of procedure parameters is reasonable considering, for example, a procedure `Graph` which allows to plot a particular function on the screen. In such a case it is desirable to parameterize the function to be plotted. In PASCAL procedure parameters must be introduced by a special symbol: `procedure` signals a formal procedure symbol, and `function` a formal function symbol. The above mentioned `Graph` procedure can then be given in PASCAL (ISO or ANSI standard) as

```
procedure Graph      (function func(x: real): real;
                      y: real);
```

by which we now have the possibility to plot any function (with one real parameter and a real result) using the `Graph` procedure.

According to the original PASCAL report (similar to ALGOL 60 or FORTRAN, for example) the number and types of the parameters of the passed procedure must not be specified, what makes static type checking impossible – especially when using separate compilation. As a consequence, the ISO and ANSI standards of PASCAL require that formal procedure parameters must be fully specified with all their own parameters and in case of a function additionally with its result type. Thus, dynamic type checking for procedure calls containing formal procedure parameters is no longer necessary. In MODULA-2 this problem is solved by providing *procedure types* as introduced in Chapter 3.4. A MODULA-2 type definition

```
TYPE  func  =  PROCEDURE (REAL) : REAL;
```

allows the specification of a procedure type, having one real parameter and producing a result of type real. The above given PASCAL example can then be formulated in MODULA-2 as

```
procedure Graph (f: func; y: real);
```

which means that a procedure of type `func` is passed to `Graph`. MODULA-2 allows only global procedures (i.e. those declared in the outermost program block) to be passed as parameters. This approach allows static type checking of the procedure (and its parameters) to be passed.

ADA does not allow to pass subprograms as parameters. Instead it provides the concept of generic program units which is explained in Chapter 5.5.

5.4   Overloading

The term overloading was already introduced in the discussion of elementary operators associated with (simple) data types. Like operators, procedures are said to be *overloaded*, if their meaning depends on the type of the arguments (i.e. the parameters). They are useful in situations, where we want to define the same conceptual operation on parameters of different types. Subprogram overloading can be found in ADA, C++, or ALGOL 68, for instance. The following declarations give an example for subprogram overloading (ADA syntax).

```
procedure INCREMENT (A: in out INTEGER; B: in INTEGER) is
begin
    A := A + B;
end;

procedure INCREMENT (A: in out FLOAT; B: in FLOAT) is
begin
    A := A + B;
end;
```

From a compiler writer's point of view the problem of overloaded operators or overloaded procedures is the same. The arguments of an overloaded operator determine the selection of the appropriate instructions, while the parameters of an overloaded procedure determine which procedure should actually be called. For example, a statement sequence

```
X := 4.5;
INCREMENT (X, 1.0);
```

contains a call of the second INCREMENT procedure, while a call of the first INCREMENT procedure is given by the sequence

```
Y := 4;
INCREMENT (Y, 1);
```

Obviously, the type information of parameters (or arguments) must allow an unambiguous choice between several possible meanings. A call of an overloaded procedure which does not exactly match the parameter structure (i.e. types and order)

of one of the appropriate procedure declarations, is somehow ambiguous and, therefore, treated as illegal.

5.5   Generic Concepts

In the preceding section we introduced the concept of overloaded procedures, which allows to have the same procedure name with different parameter structures, e.g. different types of parameters. The usage of an overloaded procedure name is restricted according to the defined declarations, of course. But in certain situations it might be desired to specify an algorithm which, then, can be used with data of arbitrary types. For example, the sorting of a list of elements can be done applying a certain algorithm, no matter whether the elements to be sorted are characters, numbers or something else. A similar problem is the handling of a queue according to a particular strategy, it does not depend on the type of the objects to be queued. Several programming languages, such as CLU or ADA, provide for those purposes *generic concepts*, allowing parameterization of types.

In ADA a *generic procedure* is a template for a class of procedures which cannot be invoked, but must be instantiated at compile time (i.e. instances of the generic procedure must be produced) to get an actual procedure. An example for the declaration of a generic procedure in ADA can be given as follows:

```
generic
type   ELEMENT is private;
type   SLIST is array (1..20) of ELEMENT;
procedure  GEN_SORT (L: in out SLIST) is
     ...
begin
     ...
end;
```

showing the generic definition of a sort procedure. The parameter of the sort procedure is a vector of type ELEMENT. The type ELEMENT is the parameter of the generic sort procedure which at compile time must be instantiated. This instantiation of the given generic procedure can be done by

```
procedure SORT_INT is new GEN_SORT (INTEGER);
```

to sort integers, or

```
procedure SORT_CHAR is new GEN_SORT (CHARACTER);
```

to sort characters. These two instantiations can be seen as two distinct procedures (because of different parameter structures) which perform the same algorithm on different data objects of different types.

In conclusion, the effect of generic procedures is to bind the formal parameters not at declaration time to a certain type. Although this effect could also be obtained with a dynamic binding concept (i.e. formal parameters are dynamically bound to actual parameters at run-time, see e.g. SMALLTALK), the generic concept should be preferred, since it allows static type checking. Certainly, the generic approach creates a copy of the code for each instantiation of a generic procedure, while with the dynamic binding concept only a single copy of the code is necessary.

5.6   Procedure Implementation

The principle actions associated with a procedure call/return mechanism are as follows:

- The status of the calling program unit must be saved.

- Storage for local variables must be allocated.

- Parameters must be passed according to the applied method.

- Access links to non-local variables must be established.

- Control must be transfered to the called procedure, e.g. loading the address of the first instruction of the procedure.

- Before terminating, local values must be moved to actual parameters according to passing methods.

- Storage for local variables must be deallocated.

- Control must be transfered back to the calling unit, e.g. restoring the address of the instruction that must be returned to on leaving the procedure.

In Section 2.4 activation records have already been introduced as data blocks (not code blocks) associated with a program unit containing information which is particular for a specific activation of that program unit. Activation records are used to manage the above mentioned actions (especially in ALGOL-like languages where it is possible to have several instances of a procedure's activation record at a time; it was already pointed out that the static structure of FORTRAN – no recursive procedures are allowed – can be handled in an easier way).

A typical *activation record* (according to Section 2.4) is shown in Figure 5.6.

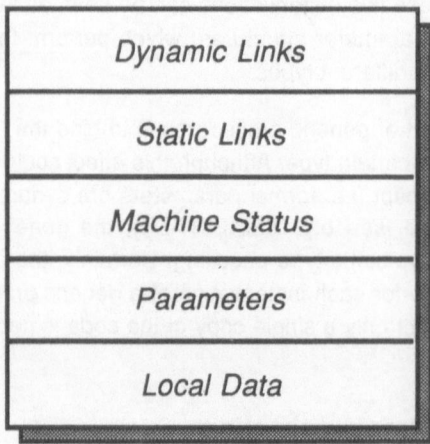

Fig. 5.6. A typical activation record

A procedure call – or the activation of a procedure – results in the *dynamic genera-tion* of such an activation record, the format of which is specified at compile time. Since the idea of a procedure is to suspend the execution of the calling program unit until the called unit terminates, it is obvious to use a *stack* to control this mech-anism. This means, with a procedure call a generated activation record is pushed onto the stack and with its termination the activation record is popped off the stack. This is done for every new activation of a procedure no matter whether it is recur-sive or not and, therefore, the procedure's local variables, for instance, can be found at different memory addresses for each activation.

This strategy is exemplified by considering the program segment of Figure 5.7 con-taining recursively defined procedures. The contents of the run-time stack is traced in Figure 5.8a to Figure 5.8e. A possible sequence of procedure calls in the program segment of Figure 5.7 could be P3 P1 P2 P2.

In Figure 5.8 the activation record of the main program (Dynsto) and the actually called procedures is shown for each state of the sequence P3 P1 P2 P2. Figure 5.8 e shows clearly that each incarnation of a recursively defined procedure has its own activation record, and therefore always the most recently defined variables in procedure P2 – i.e. those variables, which belong to the actual incarnation of P2 – will be accessed.

```
PROGRAM   Dynsto;
VAR  x, y :   INTEGER;

   PROCEDURE P1;
   VAR   x, y :   INTEGER;

      PROCEDURE P2;
      VAR  k : INTEGER;

      BEGIN

         ...  P2;  ...

      END;

   BEGIN

      ...  P2;  ...

   END;

   PROCEDURE P3;
   VAR  i :   INTEGER

   BEGIN

      ...  P1;  ...

   END;

BEGIN

      ...  P3;  ...

END.
```

Fig. 5.7. Program segment with recursive procedures

Fig 5.8a shows the stack containing only the activation record of the program unit Dynsto.

Figure 5.8b to Figure 5.8e show the stack after each procedure call. If considering the figures in reverse order one sees the contents of the stack after terminating the particular procedures. The activation records of the procedures contain the information shown in Figure 5.6. The static and dynamic links are explained in the following.

Activation record for Dynsto

Fig. 5.8a.   Stack before calling P3

Activation record for P3
Activation record for Dynsto

Fig. 5.8b.   Stack after calling P3

Activation record for P1
Activation record for P3
Activation record for Dynsto

Fig. 5.8c.   Stack after calling P1

Activation record for P2
Activation record for P1
Activation record for P3
Activation record for Dynsto

Fig. 5.8d.   Stack after calling P2 from P1

Activation record for P2
Activation record for P2
Activation record for P1
Activation record for P3
Activation record for Dynsto

Fig. 5.8e.   Stack after calling P2 recursively

Transfer of control is not the only thing which must be done, when terminating a procedure, there is also the stack, which has to be reorganized, i.e. the procedure's activation record must be released. The removal of an activation record is supported by the *dynamic link*, which is the base address of the calling program unit's activation record within the stack. The chain of dynamic links is referred to as *dy-namic chain*. It is called dynamic because it represents the dynamic structure in which procedures are activated. The dynamic chain of Figure 5.8e is shown in Figure 5.9, it shows that each activation record has a link to the activation record of its calling program unit (especially the activation record of the first call of P2 has a link to the activation record of P1, while that of the second call of P2 has a link to the activation record of the first call of P2).

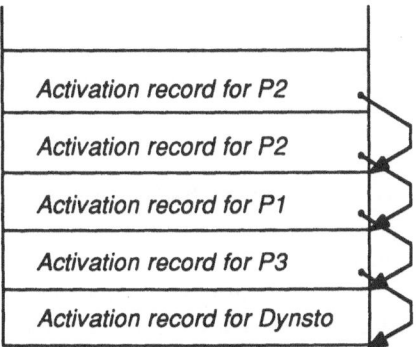

Fig. 5.9. Dynamic chain belonging to Figure 5.8e

Since procedures should not only have access to their local variables, but also to non-local variables of their context (i.e all variables of the surrounding blocks), the actually accessible variables must be defined. This is usually done by using a *static link*, which is the base address of the activation record forming the environment of the procedure. The chain of static links is referred to as *static chain*. It is called static because it reflects the static nesting structure of program units or procedures in the source code. Clearly, the static chain is in general different from the dynamic chain (especially when considering recursive procedures).

The static chain of Figure 5.8e is shown in Figure 5.10. It shows that the static link of both, the activation record of P3 and P1, is the address of the activation record of the main program Dynsto, because both procedures are declared on the same level in the declaration part of Dynsto. The static link of both incarnations of P2 must be the activation record of P1, since P2 is declared within the block of program unit P1. Access to variables of the outermost block from P2 is then given by the chain of links from P2's activation record to that of P1 and from this to the activation record of Dynsto.

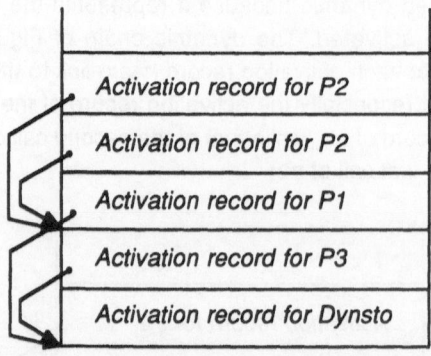

Fig. 5.10.   Static chain belonging to Figure 5.8e

A static link of a given program unit references the activation record of the statically surrounding program unit and, therefore, allows the access to non-local variables. In case of such an access to non-local variables the compiler generates code to follow an appropriate number of static links (obviously, the compiler can generate such a code, since the nesting structure of a source code is static and known at compile-time). Then, when the correct activation record has been found, the desired variable can be accessed via an offset from the corresponding base address. This can be very time consuming when the nesting level is accordingly deep.

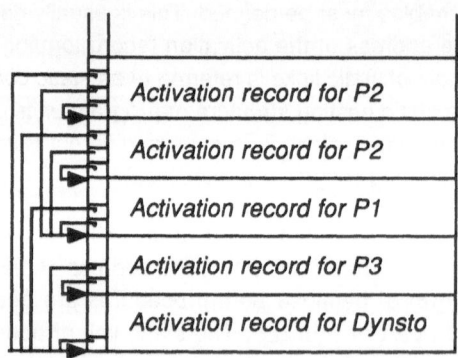

Fig. 5.11.   Displays belonging to Figure 5.8e

An alternative to handle the access to non-local variables will be given by introducing a so-called *display* whenever storage for an activation record is allocated from the stack. A display is simply a vector or table of pointers to those activation records containing accessible variables. Thus, a display is just another representation of the static chain. A display will be initialized by copying the calling program unit's display to the display of the called program unit; additionally the base address of the calling unit will be entered to the new display. Accessing a non-local variable is done via an offset from the corresponding base address which is found in the display. The display can be a part of a program unit's activation record, i.e. it is stored on the stack. But there are other possibilities to keep the display. If there is an acceptable number of registers available, then these registers might be used to maintain the display. It must be mentioned that in this case the maximum nesting depth of the source code will be limited according to the number of available registers. Other possibilities to maintain displays are discussed in [FISC 88], for example. Applying displays to the situation of Figure 5.8e is shown in Figure 5.11.

Figure 5.12 shows a program fragment with several nested procedures and appropriate procedure calls together with a trace of the stack. The program consists of the procedures p1, p2, p3, and p4; a possible sequence of procedure calls is:

    p1   p3   p4   p2

the main program calls first procedure p1, p1 calls p3, which itself calls p4, and, finally, p4 calls p2. The contents of the stack after the call of procedure p2 from p4 is shown in Figure 5.12.

The main program is (for sake of simplicity) represented by a very simple activation record (AR) consisting only of the variable x. The activation records of the procedures show entries for the corresponding local variables, the appropriate machine status, as well as the dynamic and static links.

When executing the statement

    i := j*k - x;

in procedure p2, the involved variables are accessed in the following way:

i)   Variable i is found in the activation record of procedure p2.

ii) Variable j is not found in p2's activation record, thus, we follow the static link to the activation record of procedure p1, where we find variable j.

iii) Variable k is found analogously to variable j.

iv) Variable x is neither found in p2's, nor in p1's activation record. Thus, we follow the static link to the activation record of the main program, where we find variable x.

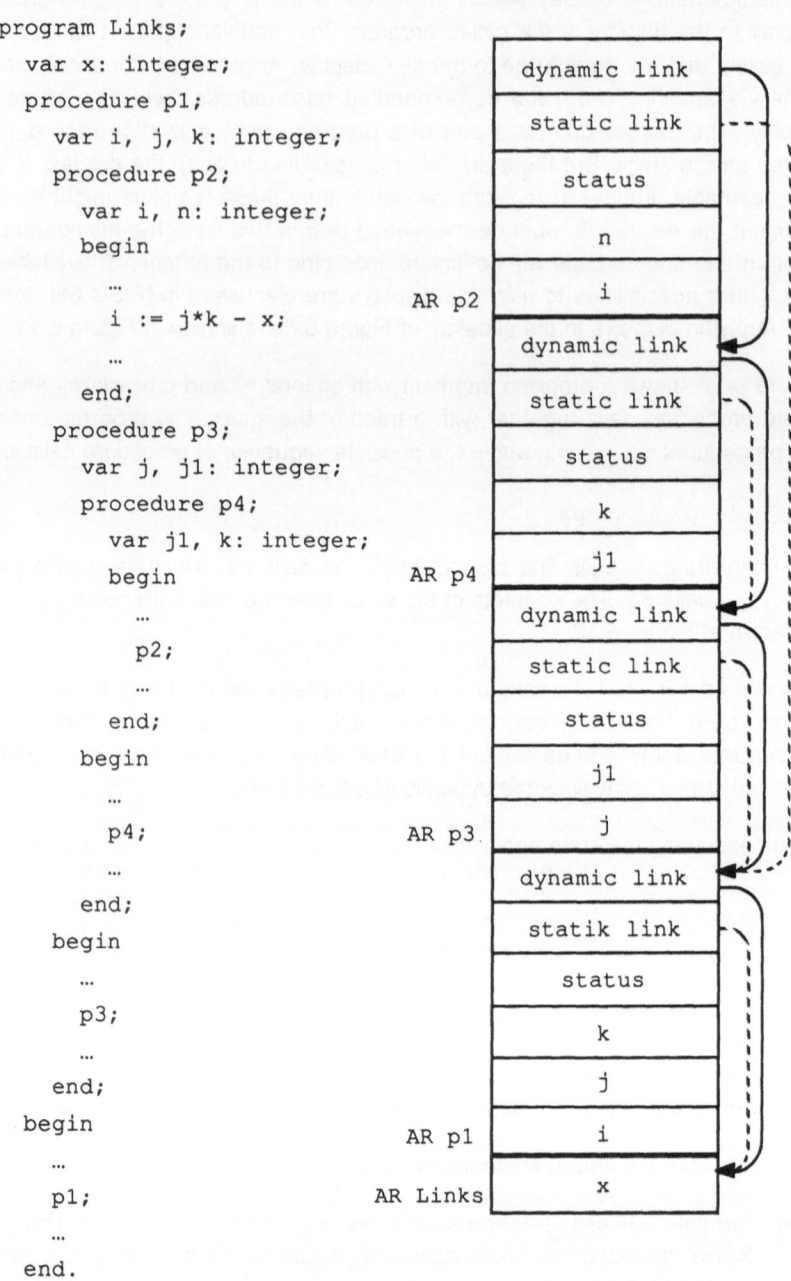

```
program Links;
    var x: integer;
    procedure p1;
        var i, j, k: integer;
        procedure p2;
            var i, n: integer;
            begin
                ...
                i := j*k - x;
                ...
            end;
        procedure p3;
            var j, j1: integer;
            procedure p4;
                var j1, k: integer;
                begin
                    ...
                    p2;
                    ...
                end;
            begin
                ...
                p4;
                ...
            end;
        begin
            ...
            p3;
            ...
        end;
    begin
        ...
        p1;
        ...
    end.
```

Fig. 5.12.   Stack trace of a procedure call sequence

6 Data Encapsulation

In Section 3.5 it was already mentioned, that data and the appropriate operations should be grouped together (i.e. *encapsulated*), and that implementation details of both, the data as well as the operations, should be hidden to the users. In this Chapter we introduce the basic ideas of data encapsulation (and therefore of abstract data types) before we consider certain abstraction techniques in SIMULA 67, C++, EIFFEL, MODULA-2, and ADA.

6.1   Abstraction, Information Hiding, and Encapsulation

The concept of *abstraction* is very powerful in programming. It allows us to focus on the operations which we want to perform without directly formulating implementation details. Procedures and functions as introduced in the preceding Chapter represent a fundamental concept of abstraction in programming languages. The occurrence of a procedure call allows to specify the execution of a sequence of statements just by the procedure's name – this name represents what has to be done, it is not of interest how it is done. Procedures are a form of *control abstraction* supporting the design and implementation process of algorithms for a given problem.

Such a procedure abstraction allows to consider the actions that have to be performed for a certain problem. However, a problem's solution means not only to perform certain actions, but also to consider the problem's data requirements. *Data abstraction* – as the second basic and also very powerful abstraction concept – allows us to focus on the data and the operations to be performed on that data without directly providing implementation details, i.e. details about the data representation in memory, as well as details on how the operations should be realized. It represents the concept of grouping together data types and appropriate operations on objects of these types as one syntactical unit and by doing this, hiding the implementation details to those applying these types and operations.

Programming languages such as MODULA-2 provide certain features allowing a jointly abstraction of data and operations, for example the concept of *modules* in MODULA-2 or *packages* in ADA. The fundamental concept is simple: Objects declared locally within a (implementation) module can only be used by the assigned procedures. Thus, the implementation of a data type, for example, is absolutely *private* to that module. Other modules are only allowed to use (not to manipulate) the features as they are provided (i.e. exported) by an interface, e.g. represented as a *definition module* considering MODULA-2. Obviously, the implementation can be changed without any problems as long as the changes does not affect the interface. Such a change in the implementation can be exemplified considering a floating-point arithmetic which might be simulated by software. Now, assume that in the future the floating-point arithmetic will directly be supported by hardware. This means that the implementation of a floating-point data type will change, but those using the type and the operations do not have to change their programs.

Parnas described this method as *information hiding* [PARN 71], [PARN 72]. The advantages of the method can easily be exemplified by the following: Assume a (very simple) bank providing the operations: Cashless money transfer; Deposit of cash; Withdrawal of cash; Checking the balance. A customer can trigger these operations either at the counter or by mail, without knowing about the bank's internal organization. For the customer it does not count, whether his money is kept in a certain drawer, or whether it is kept together with all other money, and whether the links to the accounts are provided by a simple bookkeeping. Now, assume that customers know about the internal organization of the bank, and that they have the possibility of direct access, i.e. the self-service of deposit and withdrawal of cash to/from accounts. Then, possible problems are:

- To establish the reason for inconsistencies.

- Even if assuming that the customers are honest and are working perfect, the method wouldn't work if something has to be changed in the bank's internal organization, because an enormous number of customers must be informed about these changes and the consideration of the changes must be controlled.

Considering large programming systems or software projects where all data are public, we will find the same situation, i.e. it would be impossible to verify whether the data is only used in a correct way or whether it is manipulated in an unallowed and incorrect way. Manipulations such as changes in the representation can cause severe problems in large software projects where usually a great number of programmers work together. Thus, the advantage of data encapsulation and information hiding as described above is obvious: There is no possibility for improper manipulations and, if it is necessary to change or to modify the representation of a data type, this can be done easily in a controlled way affecting only the (encapsulated) subprograms which manipulate the data type.

The programming language SIMULA 67 was the first language providing encapsulation techniques by the *class* construct, which is the first step towards abstract data types. More recently other languages such as MODULA-2, ADA, or C++ and EIFFEL followed, providing all features to define abstract data types.

The introduced concepts can best be exemplified in different programming languages using the queue example, as it will be shown for SIMULA 67, C++, EIFFEL, MODULA-2, and ADA in the following. A queue is a data abstraction which can be used to simulate certain situations, e.g. passengers waiting at an airline check-in counter, cars waiting to be filled at a filling station, or simply processes within a computer system waiting for some services such as the availability of a printer. Obviously, different strategies exist on how elements can be inserted to and/or removed from the queue. In the example we consider a so-called *FIFO queue* (first-in-first-out). A LIFO queue (last-in-first-out) would simulate a stack. The specification of the abstract data type queue is assumed to be given as follows (assuming a MODULA-2 implementation, i.e. the specification might slightly differ for other languages):

- *Elements*: A queue Q is a set of elements E, all of which are of the same data type. Both, the type of E as well as the type of Q must be available to other users to allow variable declarations of these types.

- *Strategy*: The time of arrival specifies the order of the elements of a queue. Elements are inserted at the rear of a FIFO queue and they are removed from the front of a FIFO queue, i.e. this element which has been waiting the longest for service will be removed. The queue is organized as a circular buffer.

- *Operators*: Operations are necessary to insert and remove elements, and to test whether the queue is empty or full.
  Insert: Insert an element E at the rear of a queue Q, if and only if Q is not full. No changes to Q if Q is full. Indicate the success of the operation, i.e. a parameter succ is TRUE if insert was done, FALSE otherwise. Parameters: Q, E, succ.
  Remove: The element on front of a queue Q is copied to E and then deleted, if and only if Q is not empty. No changes to E if Q is empty. Indicate the success of the operation, i.e. a parameter succ is TRUE if remove was done, FALSE otherwise. Parameters: Q, E, succ.
  IsEmpty: TRUE if queue Q is empty, FALSE otherwise. Parameter: Q.
  IsFull: TRUE if queue Q is full, FALSE otherwise. Parameter: Q.

The following Sections are based on this specification.

6.2   Classes in SIMULA 67

As already mentioned, the class construct of SIMULA 67 was the first programming language facility allowing encapsulation. Classes in SIMULA 67 are declared – like procedures or other program attributes – in the declaration part of a block. A class declaration can occur wherever a procedure declaration can occur (SIMULA 67 is a block oriented language having some similarities to the language ALGOL 60). The general form of a class declaration is very similar to a procedure declaration:

```
CLASS heading ;
    parameter specification

BEGIN
    declarations
    statements
END
```

where the `heading` contains the name of the class and formal parameters which are specified in the `parameter specification`. The class body represents a normal block which, therefore, could contain a declaration part (`declarations`) with variable, procedure or class declarations, for example.

Classes have certain similarities to generic procedures in ADA, because a class is just a template of an object which must be instantiated. Instances of classes can arbitrarily be created; they are referenced indirectly through a pointer. Classes may enclose data type definitions as well as procedures acting as operators on data objects of that type. Thus, the class construct is the encapsulation mechanism for abstract data types.

But it must be noted that the demand for hiding implementation details of data types and operations on data types is not fulfilled in SIMULA 67. All the attributes of a class can be accessed from outside similarly to the fields in PASCAL-records. Thus, local variables are visible to other program units. However, some SIMULA 67 implementations provide options for making attributes either read-only or completely hidden, allowing really abstract definitions [HEXT 90].

In the following the example of a queue data type represented by the CLASS QADT is given. As already mentioned, there are slight differences to the above given specification, e.g. in the parameter structure of the operators.

```
CLASS QADT (max);

COMMENT ** implementation of a queue and appropriate;
COMMENT ** operations;
COMMENT ** Author: B. Teufel

INTEGER max;
BEGIN
  COMMENT  ** definition of the class variables;
  COMMENT  ** i.e. the queue and related variables;

  INTEGER ARRAY queue (1:max);
  INTEGER front, rear, items;

  COMMENT  ** the operators;

  BOOLEAN PROCEDURE IsEmpty;
  COMMENT  ** true if queue is empty, false otherwise;
  BEGIN
    IsEmpty := items == 0;
  END;

  BOOLEAN PROCEDURE IsFull;
  COMMENT  ** true if queue is full, false otherwise;
  BEGIN
    IsFull := items >= max;
  END;

  PROCEDURE Insert (el, succ);
  COMMENT ** inserts el in queue if queue is not full;
  COMMENT ** success or failure is indicated by succ;
  INTEGER el;
  BOOLEAN succ;
  BEGIN
    succ := FALSE;
    IF  NOT IsFull  THEN
    BEGIN  COMMENT ** insert el at the rear of the queue;
      rear := MOD(rear, max) + 1;
      queue(rear) := el;
      item := item + 1;
      succ := TRUE;
    END;
  END;
```

```
      PROCEDURE Remove (el, succ);
      COMMENT ** copies first in queue to el and removes it;
      COMMENT ** from queue if queue is not empty;
      COMMENT ** success or failure is indicated by succ;
      INTEGER el;
      BOOLEAN succ;
      BEGIN
        succ := FALSE;
        IF  NOT IsEmpty  THEN
        BEGIN  COMMENT ** remove el at the front of the queue;
          el := queue(front);
          front := MOD(front, max) + 1;
          item := item - 1;
          succ := TRUE;
        END;
      END;

      COMMENT ** initialization (replaces a create procedure);

      items := 0;
      front := 1;
      rear := max;
    END;
```

Instances of classes are called objects in SIMULA 67 (cf [BIRT 73]). Similarly to the instantiation of pointer variables in PASCAL, for example, in SIMULA 67 we find features to define pointer variables (or reference variables in SIMULA 67 terminology) as well as features to instantiate them:

```
    REF (QADT) Q1;
```

defines the qualified reference variable Q1, i.e. pointer variables are bound to a certain class, similarly to type binding of pointer variables in other languages (cf Chapter 3), while

```
    Q1 :- NEW QADT(100);
```

instantiates a class object, i.e. a new incarnation of the above defined class is generated with a maximum size of 100 for the queue, appropriate storage is allocated, and the initialization part of the class is executed. (Note that SIMULA 67 introduces special operators for reference variables, e.g. : – denotes a reference assignment, instead of the usual assignment symbol : =.) SIMULA 67 does not provide features for explicit storage deallocation (e.g. a dispose function), since it provides an automatic garbage collector to return storage which is no longer used.

The access to class attributes from other program units has the general form

object-reference.attribute-identifier

Thus,

```
Q1.Insert(el1,si);
```

inserts element `el1` to `Q1.queue`, if `Q1.items` < `max` and the success of the operation is returned in `si`, while

```
Q1.IsEmpty;
```

tests whether `Q1.queue` is empty or not. The major problem in standard implementations is that all local variables are visible to other program units and, therefore, that those can be manipulated by every other program unit. For example, the legal assignments

```
Q1.items := 0;
```

or

```
Q1.front := 10;
```

manipulate the queue in an undesired way, i.e. the first statement actually empties the queue, while the second puts the front of the queue to an arbitrary position. Therefore, it is obvious what problems can occur, because the demand for hidden information for an abstraction is not fulfilled.

Another disadvantage of SIMULA 67 is that it provides no features for user defined data types as it can be seen in the above given example. Thus, considering strictly the definition of abstract data types, SIMULA 67 is not a language allowing abstract data types. However, it must be noted that SIMULA 67 was the first programming language providing encapsulation techniques and, therefore, it can be seen as the first step in the evolution of programming languages towards abstract data types.

It should be mentioned here that classes in SIMULA 67 can not only be defined and used as shown in the above given simple example, it is also possible to define class hierarchies. This means that a class can be defined to be a child of another class, and by this the child *inherits* the attributes of the parent – a feature which is important for object-oriented programming languages. The concept of inheritance is explained in more detail in Chapter 7.

6.3   Classes in C++

C++ can be considered as a superset of the programming language C; an introduction to C++ can be found in [STRO 86], for example. The key concept in C++ is
the user-defined data type which is called *class*. Classes in C++ show great re-
semblance to the module construct in MODULA-2: A class definition consists of

- a *public part* which, like the MODULA-2 definition module, serves as an
  interface to the users of the class (i.e. the data type);

- a *private part* which, like the MODULA-2 implementation module, holds
  the actual representation and implementation of data types and appropriate operations.

A class in C++ differs from a structure in C in that functions can be class attributes.
Then, those functions can, for example, represent certain operators. The principle
form of a class declaration is given as follows:

```
class   name   {
     members
   public:
     members
  }
```

where *name* specifies a new type name and *members* represents the declaration
of data, functions, classes, etc. Functions, for example, are then called member
functions, and as they are declared within a class they are explicitly connected to
that class (e.g. to manipulate the data objects of the class). The keyword public
controls the visibility of class members, i.e. those class members following the public keyword can be used in other program units. But public must not occur in a
class declaration, in such a case all class members are private and can not be
used by other program units.

C++ knows beside classes another form of aggregation: the structure (struct). A
structure is a class with all members public. A private keyword allows then to declare structure members to be private, reverse to the public keyword in classes.
Thus, structures and classes can be used for the same purpose. The only difference is that structure members are public by default and must be explicitly declared
private, if desired, while class members are private by default and must be explicitly
declared public, if desired.

The following gives an idea on how the above mentioned queue problem can be
solved using C++. C programmers usually "modularize" programming systems by

collecting external declarations of variables and functions in a separate file, which is historically called header file (with a suffix .h), and include that file at the front of an appropriate source file (using #include ...). The header file can be seen as the user interface which is represented by a definition module in MODULA-2. As in MODULA-2 there exists an implementation file (with a suffix .c). These are conventions, which are not part of the C or C++ language definition (unlike to MODULA-2), but it is a custom practice. Thus, the queue example can be represented by a QADT.h file (the interface), and a QADT.c file (the implementation).

The header file QADT.h :

```
/* definition of an abstract data type queue */
/* Author: B. Teufel                         */

const   int max = 100;
class   queue  {
     queue () { items = 0; front = 1; rear = max; }
     int   front, rear, items;
     int   q [max];
  public:
     int   IsEmpty ();
           /* true if queue is empty, false otherwise */
     int   IsFull ();
           /* true if queue is full, false otherwise */
     void Insert (int, int);
           /* inserts the 1st parameter in q, if q is
               not full; success or failure is indicated
               by the 2nd parameter   */
     void Remove (int, int);
           /* copies first in q to 1st parameter and removes
               it from q, if q is not empty; success or
               failure is indicated by the 2nd parameter   */
};
```

The class declaration contains a so-called *constructor* which is a member function to initialize the private data objects item, front and rear. Such a constructor must have the same name as its class. Only the operators are declared to be public and, therefore, can be used by other program units. These operators are also given as member functions, consequently they can be invoked only for variables of type queue. Since the implementation of these member functions is given separately they must be qualified using the *scope resolution operator* : :, as shown in the following.

The implementation file QADT.c :

```
#include  <QADT.h>
/* implementation of an abstract data type queue */
/* Author: B. Teufel                             */

int queue::IsEmpty ()  {
    return items == 0;
}

int queue::IsFull ()  {
    return items >= max
}

void queue::Insert (int el, int succ)  {
    succ = 0;
    if  !IsFull  {
        /* insert el at the rear of the queue */
        rear = (rear % max) + 1;
        q[rear] = el;
        ++items;
        succ = 1;
    }
}

void queue::Remove (int el, int succ)  {
    succ = 0;
    if  !IsEmpty  {
        /* remove el at the front of the queue */
        el = q[front];
        front = (front % max) + 1;
        --items;
        succ = 1;
    }
}
```

Other program units have just to include the file QADT.h for the declaration of queue variables. For example, consider the following file QADTUse.c

```
#include  <QADT.h>
        ...
main  {
    queue  q1;
        ...  ...
}
```

An `include` statement is interpreted by a C or C++ preprocessor to be replaced by the contents of the appropriate file, in the above given example the `include` statement is replaced by the contents of the file `QADT.h`. Thus, the declaration of the `class queue` is made visible in the file `QADTUse.c`. By

```
queue   q1;
```

a variable `q1` is declared to be a data object of type `queue`. Members of a class object are accessed using the dot notation (in `QADTUse.c` only public members of the type `queue` can be accessed, of course), as for example in

```
if  !q1.IsFull  {
       q1.Insert (el1,si);
       ...
}
```

it is tested whether the queue represented by `q1` is full, and if not the element `el1` is inserted to the queue `q1.q`. The success of the insert operation is returned in `si`. Differently to the situation shown for SIMULA 67, sensitive variables, such as `q1.items` or `q1.front`, cannot be accessed in other modules than the implementation module itself.

C++ provides by the introduced concepts features to define abstract data types. "A `class` is a user-defined type" [STRO 86]. The privacy concept together with separately compilable program units fulfil the demand of abstract data types for information hiding, i.e. the visibility of class members to program units outside the class can be controlled using the keywords `public` and `private`. However, the features are somehow weak in terms of header files, representing the interface to an abstract data type, and the corresponding implementation file. The problem seems to be founded on the strong influence of C to C++. A much more elegant and consistent solution was introduced by MODULA-2, as shown in Section 6.5.

6.4   Classes in EIFFEL

EIFFEL is a programming language and environment which was designed on the object-oriented paradigm to achieve reusability and extendibility. It has certain properties in common with languages, such as SIMULA 67, SMALLTALK, or C++. Detailed information about EIFFEL can be found in [MEYE 87], [MEYE 88], or [MEYE 90], for example.

EIFFEL is a strongly typed language having a syntax which is close to that of PASCAL and ADA. In EIFFEL the basic modular unit is the *class* representing the implementation of an abstract data type. Using the EIFFEL terminology an entity is a variable of such an abstract data type which can be associated with an object, i.e.

an instance of a certain class. A class, say X1, is used within another class, say X2, whenever X2 contains the declaration of a variable, i.e. an entity, of type X1:

```
e :   X1;
```

Then, class X2 is said to be a client of class X1, and X1 is said to be a supplier of X2. A class definition consists of two major clauses:

- *export*, listing all features which are available to the clients of the class;

- *feature*, describing the features of the class which are routines (or operations) and attributes, being data items associated with objects of the
  class.

Similar to MODULA-2, only the exported features are available to clients of the class. Not exported features are said to be secret. The principle form of a class declaration is given as follows:

```
class   name   export
      export list
   feature
      feature list
end; -- class name
```

where *name* specifies a new class, i.e. an abstract data type. The feature list represents secret and non-secret features. The latter are included to the export list which
controls the visibility of the features of the class. The language provides the prede-
fined feature Create to associate an entity with an object. Only after applying the
Create feature to the entity, one can make use of the features defined in the corresponding class. To access a feature, the dot notation is used:

```
entity-name.feature-name;
```

Feature-routines are of the form

```
feature-name (parameters): feature-type   is
do
      routine-body
end; -- feature name
```

where parameters and feature-type are optional. If the feature-type is specified
the feature is similar to a function, otherwise it can be understood as a procedure. A
declaration, such as

```
rear :   INTEGER;
```

within the feature clause is said to be an attribute. The type given in an attribute can be either INTEGER, REAL, CHARACTER, BOOLEAN, or a class. Constant attributes are given by a clause like the following:

```
max :   INTEGER   is   100;
```

Constant attributes occupy physical space only once, while attributes occupy physical space with each appropriate object. According to the language definition attributes are automatically initialized. For instance, rear in the above given example is initialized to zero.

Back to the realization of the given queue problem. Again, we call the class to be defined QADT and the non-secret features are isempty, isfull, insert, and remove. The definition of the class is given as follows:

```
class  QADT   export
   -- Implementation of an abstract data type QADT
   -- Author: B. Teufel

   isempty, isfull, insert, remove

feature

   items : INTEGER;
   front : INTEGER;
   rear  : INTEGER;
   max   : INTEGER;
   queue : ARRAY [INTEGER];

   Create (qsize:INTEGER) is
      -- create queue providing space for qsize elements
   do
     if  qsize > 0   then
       front := 1;
       items := 0;
       rear := qsize;
       max := qsize;
       queue.Create(1, qsize)
     end; -- if
   end; --Create

   isempty : BOOLEAN  is
      -- true if queue is empty, false otherwise
   do
```

```
      Result := (items = 0)
   end; -- isempty

   isfull : BOOLEAN  is
      -- true if queue is full, false otherwise
   do
      Result := (items = max)
   end; -- isfull

   insert (el: INTEGER) is
      -- inserts el to queue, if queue is not full
   require
      not isfull
   do
      rear := position(rear);
      queue.enter(rear,el);
      item := item + 1
   end; -- insert

   remove : INTEGER is
      -- returns first and removes it from queue,
      -- if queue is not empty
   require
      not isempty
   local
      f : INTEGER
   do
      f := front;
      front := position(front);
      item := item - 1;
      Result := queue.entry(f)
   end; -- remove

   position (p : INTEGER) : INTEGER is
      -- returns the next position to insert or remove
   do
      Result := (p mod max) + 1
   end; -- position

end; -- class QADT
```

For the implementation of the remove and insert procedures we used the possibility to attribute these procedures by so-called assertions. According to the EIFFEL terminology assertions are formal properties, such as routine pre- and postconditions or class invariants. Routine preconditions are introduced using the `require` keyword, while postconditions are introduced by the keyword `ensure`.

A class in EIFFEL represents both, the implementation of an abstract data type and the interface - given by the export list - between this implementation and the clients of the class. This is different to C++ or MODULA-2, for example, were the interface to the abstract data type is clearly separated from its implementation.

Since classes are the basic program units in EIFFEL, class `QADT` will be used within another class (a client) by declaring an entity of type `QADT`:

```
q1 :   QADT;
```

Entities must explicitly be instantiated, i.e. associated with an object. This is done using a `Create` feature. For example,

```
q1.Create(100);
```

associates `q1` with a newly created object, representing a queue of size `100`. Once the instantiation has been done, all the other features of the supplier class `QADT` can be applied to `q1` using the dot notation.

As in C++, sensitive variables such as `items` or `front` cannot be directly accessed and manipulated by the clients of the class. Those variables or entities can only be manipulated in an allowed way using the exported features. They are secret to the clients of `QADT`, analogously to the not exported features, such as `position` in our example.

6.5   Abstract Data Types in MODULA-2

MODULA-2 [WIRT 88a] provides by the *module* construct a feature allowing the definition of abstract data types. A MODULA-2 program consists of a program module, representing the main program, and an arbitrary number of other modules (called *library modules*) from which the program module imports entities, such as variables, types, or procedures. Those entities used from outside must be listed in an export list of a library module (the definition module, see below) and must be listed in an import list within the module where they are used. Library modules may import further entities from several other library modules, which are then also a part of the program.

Modules in MODULA-2 can be nested, i.e. modules can contain modules (called *local modules*) which are hidden from the rest of the program. Local modules are not important in terms of abstract data types, they just allow to control the visibility of names within a program. Wirth reports that the rare usage of local modules is the reason why they are omitted in OBERON [WIRT 88b].

Library modules are represented by two syntactical units (similar to the interface and implementation part in C++) which can be separately compiled, provided the definition module is compiled first:

- The *definition module* contains only the definitions of entities, such as constants, types or procedures. Their implementation can be found in the appropriate implementation module. A definition module acts as an interface of a library module, i.e. it exports entities of a library module which then are visible to other program units or modules and, therefore, can be used by those modules.

- The *implementation module* describes how the entities listed in the definition module are actually implemented. For example, types which are not fully specified in the definition module (so-called opaque types) are specified in the implementation module. Procedures are only defined by their header (i.e. name and parameter structure and if necessary the result) in the definition module; their implementation is given in the implementation module.

Differently from C++, definition and implementation modules are a part of the MODULA-2 language definition; they have to share the same name. Program entities which are declared in an implementation module and which are not exported by the corresponding definition module are only visible within this specific implementation module. The most important difference between abstract data types in C++ and MODULA-2 is that the module is not a type constructor as the C++ class. The module is a construct for scope control.

MODULA-2 allows to hide the representation and implementation not only of procedures and functions, but also of data types by specifying and exporting only the type's name in the definition module. Such types are called *opaque* types; their representation is given in the corresponding implementation module and is not visible outside that module. A slight restriction is that opaque types must be pointer types (according to the 3rd edition of Wirth's book "*Programming in MODULA-2*"), but this is not a serious drawback since a pointer can point to any data type. This restriction is a result of separate compilation of definition and implementation modules. Consider the following situation:

```
DEFINITION MODULE A;              MODULE B;
TYPE  T;                          FROM  A   IMPORT T;
...                               VAR  z : T;
END A;                            ...
                                  END B;
```

When compiling the program module B, the compiler must allocate storage for variable z and, therefore, has to know the size of variables of type T. Since the specification of type T is hidden in the implementation module A, this size information is not accessible when compiling B. Thus, the requirement that an opaque type has to be a pointer type is obvious, since the storage requirements for pointers are known.

The advantage of the realization of opaque types as pointers is that changes in the representation of a type does not result in the recompilation of modules importing that type. These information hiding features represent together with the possibility of separate compilation an excellent feature for encapsulation.

Separate compilation requires that imports must always refer to definition modules. Therefore, it can be avoided that the recompilation of an implementation module causes the recompilation of client modules (i.e. modules which import entities from library modules). However, the change and recompilation of a definition module effects the module's clients.

The realization of the queue problem in MODULA-2 is very simple and can be given in a very clear way, as shown in the following example. We begin with the definition module.

```
DEFINITION MODULE QADT;

(* Definition of an abstract data type queue *)
(* Author: B. Teufel                         *)

CONST  max = 100;   (* maximum size of a queue *)

TYPE
        element  =  INTEGER;
        queue;    (* a FIFO queue of integer elements *)
                  (* an opaque type *)

PROCEDURE IsEmpty (q: queue) : BOOLEAN;
          (* true if queue q is empty, false otherwise *)

PROCEDURE IsFull (q: queue) : BOOLEAN;
          (* true if queue q is full, false otherwise *)

PROCEDURE CreateQ (VAR q: queue);
          (* creates an empty queue q
             initialises queue specific parameters *)

PROCEDURE DeleteQ (VAR q: queue);
          (* deletes an queue q *)
```

```
PROCEDURE Insert (el: element;
                  VAR q: queue; VAR succ: BOOLEAN);
        (* inserts el in q, if q is not full;
           success or failure is indicated in succ   *)

PROCEDURE Remove (VAR el: element;
                  VAR q: queue; VAR succ: BOOLEAN);
        (* copies first in q to el, removes it from q, if q is
        not empty; success or failure is indicated in succ   *)


END QADT.
```

This definition module contains the *opaque* type queue, which represents a FIFO queue with elements of type integer. The elements of the queue are assumed to be integers; the element type is said to be *transparent*, because its internal structure (in our example just integer) is visible outside. For more complex structures the element type has to be replaced. For example, assuming that the queue elements represent passengers waiting for certain flights of an airline, the elements could be represented as

```
element  =  RECORD
               Name        : ARRAY [1..50] OF CHAR;
               AirlineCode : ARRAY [1..3] OF CHAR;
               FlightNo    : INTEGER;
               Class       : CHAR;
                    ...
            END;
```

Additional to the previous given implementations, we find in this definition module (i.e. the specification of the abstract data type queue) a procedure CreateQ, which is used to generate an empty queue for a variable of type queue, and a procedure DeleteQ, which is used to delete a queue that is associated with a variable of type queue. The procedure CreateQ is needed, because queue is an opaque type and, therefore, is a pointer, which means that we must dynamically allocate storage for the queue structure (i.e. create a queue). Obviously, DeleteQ is used to deallocate dynamically a queue structure.

Thus, considering this definition module we actually find a declaration of an abstract data type queue, fulfilling all requirements: new types are declared and named, operations on that types are specified by procedures, and all implementation details (even those of the representation of data objects of type queue) are hidden to other program units. The corresponding implementation module is given as follows:

```
IMPLEMENTATION MODULE QADT;


(* Implementation of an abstract data type queue *)
(* Author: B. Teufel                            *)

FROM Storage IMPORT ALLOCATE, DEALLOCATE;

TYPE
    queue    =  POINTER TO QueueRec;
    QueueRec =  RECORD
                   front, rear : [1..max];
                   items       : [0..max];
                   el          : ARRAY [1..max] OF element;
                END;


PROCEDURE IsEmpty (q: queue) : BOOLEAN;
BEGIN
    RETURN q^.items = 0
END IsEmpty;


PROCEDURE IsFull (q: queue) : BOOLEAN;
BEGIN
    RETURN q^.items = max
END IsFull;


PROCEDURE CreateQ (VAR q: queue);
BEGIN
    NEW(q);
    q^.front := 1;  q^.rear := max;
    q^.items := 0;
END CreateQ;


PROCEDURE DeleteQ (VAR q: queue);
BEGIN
    DISPOSE(q);
    q := NIL;
END DeleteQ;


PROCEDURE Insert (el: element;
                  VAR q: queue; VAR succ: BOOLEAN);
BEGIN
    succ := FALSE;
    IF  NOT IsFull(q)   THEN
```

```
              (* insert el at the rear of the queue *)
              q^.rear := (q^.rear MOD max) + 1;
              q^.el[q^.rear] := el;
              INC(q^.items);
              succ := TRUE;
         END;
    END Insert;


    PROCEDURE Remove (VAR el: element;
                      VAR q: queue; VAR succ: BOOLEAN);
    BEGIN
         succ := FALSE;
         IF  NOT IsEmpty(q)  THEN
              (* remove el at the front of the queue *)
              el := q^.el[q^.front];
              q^.front := (q^.front MOD max) + 1;
              DEC(q^.items);
              succ := TRUE;
         END;
    END Remove;


    BEGIN
         (* no initializations are necessary *)
    END QADT.
```

Modules that want to use the queue type and the associated operations must import the type and operations, as in:

```
    MODULE QADTUse;

    FROM  QADT  IMPORT  queue, element, IsEmpty, IsFull,
                        CreateQ, DeleteQ, Insert, Remove;

    VAR  el : element;
         q1 : queue;
         si : BOOLEAN;

    BEGIN
         CreateQ (q1);
         ...
         Insert (el, q1, si);
         ...
         DeleteQ (q1);
    END QADTUse;
```

Imported entities are used just by referring the appropriate names. It is not necessary to import all entities which are exported by a certain module, if only a part of the modules functionality is required. In that case only the desired entities must be included in the import list. The import list can be abbreviated if all entities of a module are imported, using the form

```
IMPORT QADT;
```

Importing entities from a module in this way has effects on the name qualification, i.e. imported entities must be qualified explicitly. Considering our example, this means, for instance, that we have to use

```
QADT.CreateQ (q1);    instead of    CreateQ (q1);
```

Like in C++, sensitive variables such as $q^\wedge.items$, etc. cannot be accessed (and, thus, cannot be manipulated) by other modules than the implementation module itself. Opaque types are the only problem with abstract data types in MODULA-2. As already mentioned an opaque type must be a pointer in MODULA-2. This means that with the declaration of a variable of an opaque type only a pointer variable is defined. Therefore, an additional operation to create (or delete) the actual data structure is needed (in our example CreateQ). Now, the unsolved problem is how to be sure that the user of such a type actually creates an object of the type using the provided create function.

6.6 Abstract Data Types in ADA

The general concept for abstract data types in ADA is very similar to that of MODULA-2 discussed in the previous section. There are, of course, several syntactical differences, as well as a semantic one. As in MODULA-2 the modularization of complex problems into program units and the organization of such program units are considered to be the central issues in the construction of ADA programs.

ADA provides with the *package* construct a feature allowing the definition of abstract data types. The counterpart of the MODULA-2 definition module is in ADA the *visible part* of a package, while the implementation module has its counterpart in the *package body*. For example,

```
package COMPEX_NUMBERS is
      -- visible information
      type  COMPLEX  is
            record
                  re, im : REAL;
            end record;
   end;
```

```
package body COMPLEX_NUMBERS is
     -- bodies of visible procedures
     -- additional internal structures
     -- (not visible outside the package body)
begin
     -- initialization code
end;
```

shows a package COMPLEX_NUMBERS with its visible part and its implementation
body. As in MODULA-2, both packages share the same name.

As in other languages the visible definition of a type can cause security problems,
because users can make use of the visible information, i.e. the structure of the representation of a type. For example, one can manipulate directly the real part or
imaginary part of a data object of type COMPLEX, instead of using the provided operators. In MODULA-2 the integrity of an abstraction is guaranteed by opaque
types. The *private* concept ensures in ADA the integrity of an abstraction. The private concept means, the representation of data objects of an abstract data type is
invisible to other program units, if the type is declared to be private. Now, the major
difference between MODULA-2 and ADA (in terms of abstract data types) is that
MODULA-2, as explained above, requires that opaque types are pointer types,
while private types in ADA are not restricted. The explained size problems occurring by opaque types and separate compilation are solved in ADA by declaring a
private type twice. For example,

```
package COMPEX_NUMBERS is
     -- visible information
     type  COMPLEX  is private

private
     -- invisible information
     type  COMPLEX  is
          record
               re, im : REAL;
          end record;
end;
```

The part of the package specification before the reserved word private is the visible part which shows the information that is accessible by other program units. The
type COMPLEX is declared to be private and, therefore, implementation details are
not accessible outside the package. After the reserved word private the details of
the type COMPLEX are specified. When compiling a program unit which imports a
private type from another package, the compiler gets enough information about the
private type to determine its size.

The realization of the queue problem in ADA is very similar to the MODULA-2 realization. The package specification is given as follows:

```
package  QADT  is

-- definition of an abstract data type queue
-- Author: B. Teufel

type  QUEUE  is private;   -- a FIFO queue
type  ELEMENT  is new  INTEGER;

function ISEMPTY (Q: in QUEUE) return BOOLEAN;
          -- true if queue Q is empty, false otherwise

function ISFULL (Q: in QUEUE) return BOOLEAN;
          -- true if queue Q is full, false otherwise

procedure INSERT (EL: in ELEMENT;
                  Q: in out QUEUE; SUCC: in out BOOLEAN);
          -- inserts el in q, if q is not full;
          -- success or failure is indicated in succ

procedure REMOVE (EL: in out ELEMENT;
                  Q: in out QUEUE; SUCC: in out BOOLEAN);
          -- copies first in q to el and removes it from q,
          -- if q is not empty;
          -- success or failure is indicated in succ

private

    MAX : constant := 100;

    type  QUEUE  is
        record
            FRONT : INTEGER range 1..MAX := 1;
            REAR  : INTEGER range 1..MAX := MAX;
            ITEMS : INTEGER range 0..MAX := 0;
            EL    : array (1..MAX) of ELEMENT;
        end record;

end;
```

The above explained concept of private types is clearly exemplified in this package specification and the difference to MODULA-2 can be seen: there is no procedure

necessary to create a data object of type QUEUE, since it is not a pointer type. The
necessary initializations (e.g. ITEMS := 0) are given with the type specification in
the private part of the package.

This example shows us the declaration of an abstract data type with no restrictions:
new types can be declared and named and must not – as in MODULA-2 – be made
visible as pointer types, operations on that types are specified by procedures or
functions, and all implementation details are hidden to other program units. The
corresponding package body is given as follows:

```
package body  QADT  is

-- Implementation of an abstract data type queue
-- Author: B. Teufel

function ISEMPTY (Q: in QUEUE) return BOOLEAN  is
begin
      return (Q.ITEMS = 0);
end ISEMPTPY;

function ISFULL (Q: in QUEUE) return BOOLEAN  is
begin
      return (Q.ITEMS = MAX);
end ISFULL;

procedure INSERT (EL: in ELEMENT;
                  Q: in out QUEUE; SUCC: in out BOOLEAN)   is
begin
     SUCC := FALSE;
     if  not ISFULL(Q)  then
          -- insert el at the rear of the queue
          Q.REAR := (Q.REAR mod MAX) + 1;
          Q.EL(Q.REAR) := EL;
          Q.ITEMS := Q.ITEMS + 1;
          SUCC := TRUE;
     end if;
end INSERT;

procedure REMOVE (EL: in out ELEMENT;
                  Q: in out QUEUE; SUCC: in out BOOLEAN) is
begin
     SUCC := FALSE;
     if  not ISEMPTY(Q)  then
          -- remove el at the front of the queue
```

```
                EL := Q.EL(Q.FRONT);
                Q.FRONT := (Q.FRONT mod MAX) + 1;
                Q.ITEMS := Q.ITEMS - 1;
                SUCC := TRUE;
            end if;
    end REMOVE;


    end QATD;
```

The usage of the package is shown by the following procedure QADTUse which is going to be a main program in the usual sense. QADTUse has no parameters and it can be assumed that it can be called somehow.

```
with QADT;
use QADT;
procedure QADTUse is
   E1 : ELEMENT;
   Q1 : QUEUE;
   SI : BOOLEAN;

begin
    ...
    INSERT (E1, Q1, SI);
    if not SI then  ...
    ...
    REMOVE (E1, Q1, SI);
    ...
end QADTUse;
```

The first statement of that fragment shows the dependency to the QADT package. The *with* clause represents the import list in ADA. The difference to MODULA-2 is that the *with* clause always imports all entities of a package, while the MODULA-2 import list allows a selective import of entities. Without the following *use* statement we had to refer to entities of the QADT package using the dot notation and qualifying the package's name, e.g.

```
QADT.INSERT (E1, Q1, SI);
```

Applying the *use* clause it is not necessary to have such an explicit qualification. Thus, omitting the *use* clause we have to have an explicit qualification for the entities of a package, similar to the explicit qualification in MODULA-2 when using the abbreviated import list (i.e. using just IMPORT QADT;).

The given procedure is more or less similar to the above given MODULA-2 program QADTUse, except that there is no explicit creation of a queue object, because

private data types are not restricted to pointer types. This is an advantage over
MODULA-2. But the coin has two sides: The disadvantage is that all client modules
must be recompiled if the representation of a type changes. This can be avoided
using pointer types yielding to the MODULA-2 situation.

Important to note is that ADA provides – similar to generic procedures (cf Chapter
5) – *generic packages* and, thus, *generic abstract data types*. For example, the restriction of the above given queue type to have only 100 elements can be avoided
by declaring the following generic package which, then, can be instantiated for
another size:

```
generic
      MAX : NONNEGATIVE;
package  GEN_QADT  is


-- definition of a generic abstract data type queue
-- Author: B. Teufel


type  QUEUE  is private;  -- a FIFO queue
type  ELEMENT  is new  INTEGER;


function ISEMPTY (Q: in QUEUE) return BOOLEAN;
          -- true if queue Q is empty, false otherwise


function ISFULL (Q: in QUEUE) return BOOLEAN;
          -- true if queue Q is full, false otherwise


procedure INSERT (EL: in ELEMENT;
                    Q: in out QUEUE; SUCC: in out BOOLEAN);
          -- inserts el in q, if q is not full;
          -- success or failure is indicated in succ


procedure REMOVE (EL: in out ELEMENT;
                    Q: in out QUEUE; SUCC: in out BOOLEAN);
          -- copies first in q to el and removes it from q,
          -- if q is not empty;
          -- success or failure is indicated in succ


   private


      type  QUEUE  is
          record
              FRONT : INTEGER range 1..MAX := 1;
```

```
                REAR   : INTEGER range 1..MAX := MAX;
                ITEMS  : INTEGER range 0..MAX := 0;
                EL     : array (1..MAX) of ELEMENT;
            end record;

     end;
```

The package body is the same as before. We can now create and use a queue of a particular size by instantiating the generic package as in the following fragment:

```
     package QADT50 is new GEN_QADT (50);
     use QADT50;

         ...
         INSERT (E1, Q1, SI);
         if  not SI  then  ...
```

The behaviour of QADT50 is the same as for QADT, except that the size of the queue is instantiated by 50. The use clause has the same semantic as for normally written packages. Another instantiation, e.g.

```
     package QADT250 is new GEN_QADT (250);
```

allows to declare queues of size 250. Obviously, the generic concept cannot only be applied to the size of a queue in our example, but also to the element type, for instance (cf [BARN 89], for example). Thus, ADA allows with this generic concept a more flexible definition of abstract data types than MODULA-2 or C++, for example.

7 Inheritance

Inheritance in programming languages means the definition of new entities (e.g. types, classes or abstract data types) on the basis of existing ones and that those new entities inherit the properties of the existing ones. Thus, we find certain forms of inheritance in several imperative programming languages, although inheritance is widely understood to be a feature of object-oriented programming languages. (The evolution of object-oriented programming languages can best be followed when considering the proceedings of the Conferences on Object-Oriented Programming Systems, Languages and Applications or the European Conferences on Object-Oriented Programming, see for example [COOK 89].)

Therefore, after introducing the basic ideas of inheritance in programming languages, we start with a consideration of subranges in PASCAL and MODULA-2 and subtypes in ADA, followed by an introduction to type extension in OBERON. Thereafter, we discuss inheritance in SIMULA 67, SMALLTALK, and C++. We show by an example that inheritance does not work in the same way in all of these languages.

7.1   Basic Ideas

Objects of real world problems or concepts typically do not appear as independent entities, but relate to other concepts in a way that they can be organized using, for example, a hierarchical structure of *groups* or *classes*. Super-classes, classes, sub-classes, etc. form the hierarchy. For instance, cars, busses, and trucks relate to vehicles, which itself relate to some transportation medium. Another example can be found in office information systems, where multi-media documents can be classified in a hierarchy (see [CHRI 86]). A classification of *beers*, for example, can be given in a hierarchical structure as it is shown in Figure 7.1.

A super-class of beers could be given by drinks in general. The three main sub-classes of beers are alcoholic, light, and non-alcoholic beers. Each of these subclasses itself can be divided into other sub-classes. In the example only alcoholic beers are further sub-divided into four classes. The given hierarchical classification is based on certain properties, each of which characterizes the corresponding class. Such properties might be attributes like the *proof* or *alcoholic strength* in case of alcoholic beers, or it might be a form of operation, such as "*serve with lemon*" in case of yeast-free wheat beer.

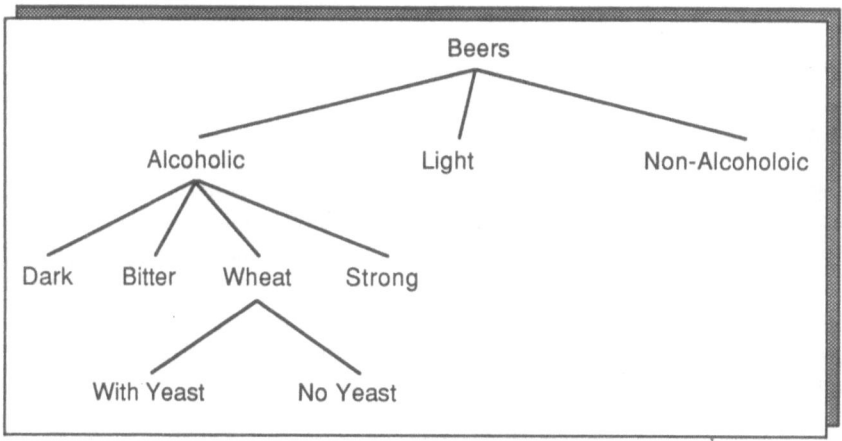

Fig. 7.1. Hierarchical classification of beers

Now, the principle idea of such a class hierarchy is that sub-classes *inherit* the properties of the corresponding super-classes. For example, a property of beers could be the operation "*serve chilled*". Thus, alcoholic beers inherit "*serve chilled*" and *proof* is added. Wheat beer inherits all these and may add the property of "*must be consumed within a certain time*", and yeast-free wheat beer inherits all those properties and additionally adds "*serve with lemon*".

- *Inheritance* in programming languages is a feature allowing the specification of a *new class of objects* on the basis of an existing class (or classes), thus, extending the previously specified class (or classes). The new class inherits properties of the existing ones.

- Subclasses are *specializations* of the corresponding superclasses. They may add to the inherited attributes and operations new attributes and operations which are appropriate to more specialized objects. Thus, a programmer must not necessarily start from scratch when dealing with similar objects and code must not be rewritten, but instead it can be reused.

The introduced example implies that each class could best be implemented by abstract data types, but in this case it is highly desirable that the programming language provides features allowing the definition of class hierarchies, and by this to inherit properties (i.e. attributes and operations) to sub-classes. Not every language providing features to specify abstract data types also provides inheritance features. Examples are given in the following Sections for SIMULA 67, SMALLTALK, and C++.

7.2   Subranges and Subtypes

Subrange types or subtypes can be considered to represent the simplest forms of inheritance in programming languages. However, those types are usually restricted to (already defined) scalar types.

While the usual type classification of data objects results in non-overlapping sets of data objects, the introduction of subranges and subtypes allows such an overlapping. For example, 'M' is a member of both sets defined by the subranges ['A'..'P'], or ['K'..'Z'], as well as a member of the set of all characters. They mainly have been introduced to allow the compiler to generate guards for assignments, e.g. to control index ranges in this way. The fundamentals of subtypes can be explained in the following way.

Let $V(T)$ be the set of values bound to type T, and $O(T)$ be the operations bound to type T. Then, the basic idea of subtypes T' corresponding to a given type T (called the supertype) is given by the following simple relationship:

$$T' \text{ is a subtype of } T \quad \Rightarrow \quad V(T') \subseteq V(T) \quad \text{and} \quad O(T') \equiv O(T)$$

This means that any data object of subtype T' is also an object of the supertype T and most of all that any operation which can be applied to objects of type T can also be applied to objects of type T'. The principle is that a data object of a subtype can occur wherever an object of the corresponding supertype can occur. Thus, the concept of inheritance is obvious: A subtype *inherits* the operations of the corresponding supertype.

Subrange types were introduced in PASCAL, and can also be found in MODULA-2 and ADA. A typical PASCAL (or MODULA-2) subrange type definition can be given by

```
type    index  =  1..20;
        lower  =  'a'..'z';
        upper  =  'A'..'Z';
```

where subrange types are allowed to be defined as subranges of any already defined scalar type by specifying the smallest and largest constant value in the subrange. We quote from [JENS 74]: "*Semantically, a subrange type is an appropriate substitution for the associated scalar type in all definitions. Furthermore, it is the associated scalar type which determines the validity of all operations involving values of subrange types".*

Subtypes in ADA are not really new types, they are used to specify objects by certain types, but with individual constraints or restrictions on their values. Using ADA syntax, the above given example looks as follows

```
subtype   index   is   INTEGER range 1..20;
subtype   lower   is   CHARACTER range 'a'..'z';
subtype   upper   is   CHARACTER range 'A'..'Z';
```

Objects belonging to different subtypes of the same type can be mixed in expressions and assignments as long as the corresponding restrictions are fulfilled. As in PASCAL or MODULA-2 the ADA subtype inherits all the operations of the corresponding supertype.

7.3   Extended Types in OBERON

The programming language OBERON [WIRT 88c] is a general purpose programming language and a direct successor of MODULA-2, resulting from Niklaus Wirth's efforts to increase the power of MODULA-2 and to decrease its complexity.

Like MODULA-2, OBERON distinguishes between implementation and definition program units, they are called *module* and *definition*, respectively. A definition belongs always to the corresponding module and represents the interface to client modules, i.e. the visible declaration part. This reflects what we know as definition modules and implementation modules in MODULA-2.

OBERON does not provide subrange types (cf [WIRT 88b]), but it provides as a new feature the facility of *extended record types*, i.e. it allows the specification of new record types on the basis of existing ones, the so-called base types. Extended types represent a hierarchic relationship to the corresponding base types. Type extension is discussed in detail in [WIRT 88d].

According to [WIRT 88b] a type T' declared by

```
T'   =   RECORD (T)
               <field definitions>
         END
```

is said to be a *direct extension* of type T, and T is said to be a *direct base type* of T'. T might already be an extended type. Thus, T' is an extension of T, if T' = T, or if T' is a direct extension of an extension of T. For example, considering the base type

```
  T  =  RECORD
              a, b : CHAR
         END
```

we can define the extension

```
  T1  =  RECORD (T)
                c : INTEGER
             END
```

allowing to define data objects with fields a, b, c.

Base types and extended types in OBERON are assignment compatible, that means that variables of an extended type can be assigned to variables of the corresponding base type. For example, assume the following variable declarations:

```
  t   :  T;
  t1  :  T1;
```

Then the following assignment is possible:

```
  t  :=  t1;
```

This assignment involves only the fields a and b, i.e.

```
  t.a := t1.a    and    t.b := t1.b.
```

The field t1.c is not involved in this assignment. The assignment represents a projection from the values of the extended types to the base type. Obviously, the reverse assignment (i.e. t1 := t) is not allowed because it does not fully specify the values of the extended type. However, this reverse assignment is allowed, if a type guard is applied to t. A *type guard* has the form

```
  t(T1)
```

(considering the above example) and it asserts that t is temporarily of type T1. Then

```
  t1 := t(T1);
```

is allowed.

The concept of extended types is similar to the class concept introduced by SIMULA 67. The properties of the base type are *inherited* to the extended type. Especially operations on a base type, represented by procedures with formal parameters of that base type, are inherited to the extended types, because – similar to the assignment compatibility – the actual parameters are allowed to be of an extended type of the corresponding base type of the formal parameters.

The separation of a module specification into an implementation and a definition part allows the combination of the concept of information hiding and that of extended types. For example, the definition could contain the following type declaration:

```
T  =  RECORD
           x, y  :  INTEGER
        END
```

and the corresponding module can extend T by some private fields:

```
T  =  RECORD
           x, y  :  INTEGER;   (* public *)
           a, b  :  INTEGER    (* private *)
        END
```

Only the type declaration in the definition is visible outside, i.e. client modules can only access the fields x and y of T, the fields a and b are hidden to clients. The visible or public part of the type declaration T is called the *public projection* of the whole type T, as defined in the corresponding module.

7.4   Inheritance in SIMULA 67

It was already explained that SIMULA 67 provides with its *class* construct not only an encapsulation facility, but also the facility of inheritance by supporting hierarchies of classes. Thus, this Section is closely related to Section 6.2, where we introduced the basic ideas of SIMULA 67 classes and the way how to declare a class. Once again we want to point out that all attributes of a class can be accessed from outside, i.e. local variables are visible to other program units.

We adapt here the introduced queue example, i.e. the CLASS QADT, from Section 6.2. The class declaration is repeated for the sake of completeness and readability, at least in an abbreviated form:

```
CLASS QADT (max);

INTEGER max;

BEGIN
   INTEGER ARRAY queue (1:max);
   INTEGER front, rear, items;
```

```
      BOOLEAN PROCEDURE IsEmpty;
      BEGIN
         ...
      END;

      BOOLEAN PROCEDURE IsFull;
      BEGIN
         ...
      END;

      PROCEDURE Insert (el, succ);
      ...
      BEGIN
         ...
      END;

      PROCEDURE Remove (el, succ);
      ...
      BEGIN
         ...
      END;
      ...
   END;
```

The declaration

```
      REF (QADT) Q1;
```

defines the qualified reference variable Q1 and

```
      Q1 :- NEW QADT(100);
```

instantiates a class object (cf Section 6.2).

Now, SIMULA 67 supports class hierarchies by allowing the definition of *sub-classes*. In order to declare a class B to be a subclass of a class A, we have to prefix B by the name A:

```
      CLASS A;
      BEGIN
            INTEGER x;
            ...
      END;
```

```
A CLASS B;
BEGIN
      INTEGER y;
      ...
END;
```

In this case B inherits all attributes and/or operations of A, i.e. with

```
REF (B) b1;
...
b1 :- NEW B;
```

we can access b1.x as well as b1.y, for example.

In our queue example we probably might be interested in an object providing the additional functionality of a lookup function to verify whether a certain element is included to the queue. This can be given as a subclass of class QADT in the following way:

```
QADT CLASS QL;
COMMENT ** implementation of a subclass of class QADT;
COMMENT ** Author: B. Teufel;

BEGIN

  BOOLEAN PROCEDURE Lookup (el);
  COMMENT ** returns true if el is in queue;
  INTEGER el;

  BEGIN

    INTEGER i;
    BOOLEAN found;
    found := FALSE;
    i := front;

    WHILE  i /= rear AND NOT found  DO
    COMMENT ** remember queue was implemented as a
    COMMENT ** circular buffer
    BEGIN
      IF  queue(i) = el  THEN  found := TRUE;
      i := MOD(i,max) + 1;
    END;
```

```
     IF   NOT found   THEN   found := queue(rear) = el;
     Lookup := found;

  END;


  END;
```

An appropriate pointer variable can be declared by

```
     REF (QL) Q1;
```

and instantiated by

```
     Q1 :- NEW QL(100);
```

where 100 matches the formal parameter of QADT. The object Q1 allows access to the following operations and attributes:

```
     Q1.max          Q1.queue        Q1.front
     Q1.rear         Q1.items        Q1.IsEmpty
     Q1.IsFull       Q1.Insert       Q1.Remove
     Q1.Lookup
```

SIMULA 67 allows to define a subclass of a subclass and, thus, allows inheritance over several levels. For example, the above given class B might have a subclass C. Then B prefixes the declaration of C:

```
     B CLASS C;
     BEGIN
          INTEGER z;

          ...
     END;
```

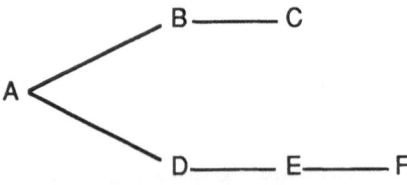

Fig. 7.2.   A class hierarchy

An appropriate reference variable c1 has access to $c1.x$, $c1.y$, and $c1.z$. Since it is allowed to define several subclasses to a given class, hierarchies of arbitrary complexity can be defined. For example, the compound object of Figure 7.2 can be specified in the following way:

```
A CLASS B;
BEGIN      ...     END;
B CLASS C;
BEGIN      ...     END;
A CLASS D;
BEGIN      ...     END;
D CLASS E;
BEGIN      ...     END;
E CLASS F;
BEGIN      ...     END
```

Let a1 be a reference variable for class A. Then, the variables of class A can be accessed by a1, e.g. a1.x. The variables of A's subclasses, however, cannot be accessed directly, they need further qualification. For this case SIMULA 67 provides the keyword QUA:

```
a1 QUA B.y
```

allows access to y by a1. But QUA can also be used when a subclass (B) and the corresponding superclass (A) contain a variable of the same name. For example, assume b1 to be a reference variable of class B, and that both, class A and class B declare a variable n. Then,

```
b1.n
```

allows access to the variable n declared in class B, while

```
b1 QUA A.n
```

allows access to variable n declared in class A.

An interesting question is how the inheritance will work. To explain this in SIMULA 67, SMALLTALK-80, and C++ we consider the following example:

```
CLASS C1;
BEGIN

      PROCEDURE alpha;
            beta;

      PROCEDURE beta;
            OUTTEXT("beta in C1");

END;
```

```
C1 CLASS C2;
BEGIN

    PROCEDURE beta;
        OUTTEXT("beta in C2");

END;
```

Class C1 consists of two procedures alpha and beta, where alpha calls beta, and beta consists just of an output procedure call. Class C2 consists only of a procedure beta. Now, assume the following situation

```
REF (C1) x;
REF (C2) y;
    ...
x :- NEW C1;
y :- NEW C2;

    ...
x.alpha;    x.beta;
y.alpha;    y.beta;
```

Object references have access to composed objects at their qualification level, where they are sought first. Outer levels follow in turn and access is given to the first corresponding object. This means, with x.alpha we refer to procedure alpha of class C1 which calls procedure beta of class C1 and, thus, the text "beta in C1" is the output. x.beta describes the same situation, while y.beta is sought and found in class C2. Thus, the output of y.beta is "beta in C2". The interesting situation is given by y.alpha. First, alpha is sought in class C2 and not found, so it is sought in the superclass, i.e. in class C1, where it is found. Thus, y.alpha invokes alpha of class C1, which itself invokes beta of C1, since it has in an unqualified way no access to entities of a subclass.

7.5   Inheritance in SMALLTALK-80

When talking about SMALLTALK-80 we talk not primarily about a programming language, but about a programming environment. Unfortunately, the SMALLTALK syntax and terminology is sometimes a bit strange and unusual. Thus, we try to give a very brief introduction to SMALLTALK terminology and concepts, before giving an example for inheritance in SMALLTALK-80. A detailed description of SMALLTALK and its usage can be found in [GOLD 83] or [SHAF 91], while an introductory overview of SMALLTALK and a comparison to other languages, such as CLU for example, is given in [KAMI 90].

The SMALLTALK-80 system was developed at Xerox-PARC. Adele Goldberg and David Robson make the following statements in the preface of their book on SMALLTALK-80 [GOLD 83]:

- *SMALLTALK is based on a small number of concepts, but defined by unusual terminology.*

- *SMALLTALK is a graphical, interactive programming environment.*

- *SMALLTALK is a big system.*

This means, a programmer has only to learn a few concepts to use the SMALL-TALK system, but he/she (probably) has to translate the usual (e.g. PASCAL) terminology into SMALLTALK terminology. However, the Xerox Learning Research Group attached great importance to the user interface of the system, thus, supporting a programmer's work by the interface: "*Every component accessible to the user should be able to present itself in a meaningful way for observation and manipulation*" [INGA 81]. Thus, the SMALLTALK-80 environment is highly interactive and provides visual communication. The system provides a great number of objects performing functions such as storage management, file handling, editing, or compiling and debugging.

The programming language SMALLTALK-80 was mainly influenced by SIMULA 67, especially the fundamental ideas of objects, messages and classes came from SIMULA 67 [XERO 81]. It is based upon the idea of user defined abstract data types with the concept of encapsulation, information hiding, and inheritance. The SMALLTALK-80 vocabulary is around the following five basic terms:

- *object*,

- *message*,

- *class*,

- *instance*, and

- *method*.

An *object* is a package of information or data and appropriate operations for manipulations (i.e. procedures) that belong together. The functionality of the operations of an object depend on the type of the data. For example, the functionality of operations of objects representing numbers is given by arithmetic functions. Objects can represent, for instance, numbers, character strings, circles, or queues, but also text editors, programs, or compilers. Particularly, constants and the contents of variables are objects. A SMALLTALK object is similar to a PASCAL record, but it is much richer and more versatile [KAEH 86].

A *message* is a request for one of an object's operations. It is syntactically represented by a message selector (i.e. a symbolic name describing the manipulation) and its operands. Messages are this medium in SMALLTALK to perform certain actions. Compared to programming languages like PASCAL, messages represent procedure calls or applying operators, etc. The basic concept in SMALLTALK-80 is that objects interact only by sending and receiving messages. Thus, the programmer has to specify the way messages are sent, as well as what has to be done when messages are received. Sending a message means to describe the receiver, the message selector, and the arguments of the message. For example,

```
alpha  +  10
```

means, the object `alpha` receives the message *arithmetic addition* with the argument `10`. On receiving a message, an object looks if the received message matches one of the messages to which it can respond. This set of respond messages is called the object's *interface*, and it describes the operations which can be invoked for that object.

A *class* is a description of a set of similar objects. In other words, a class describes an abstract data type, i.e. it describes the implementation of the individual objects of the class, as well as the appropriate operations. The SMALLTALK-80 system provides a set of classes – the *system classes* – for arithmetic, data structures, control structures, and input/output facilities. New instances of a class are created by sending the massage *new* to the class itself. The response then is a new instance of the class, i.e. an uninitialized object.

The objects which are described by a class are called the *instances* of the class. All instances of a class have the same interface, i.e. they can respond to the same messages. Beside this, instances have a private part represented by so-called *instance variables* – describing the data structure to be allocated on instantiation – and the set of operations. Both, instance variables and operations are not directly available to other objects.

A *method* can best be described by the term subprogram or procedure. It describes a sequence of actions to be executed when an appropriate message is received by an object, i.e. it describes an object's operation. Methods consist of message patterns, temporary variable names, and expressions representing the method body. The message pattern is the name of a message to which the method responds. This includes the arguments. The temporary variables are like local variables of a procedure, they exist during the execution of the method. The method body – like a procedure body – specifies the actions to be performed on responding a message.

It is difficult to give a SMALLTALK example just on paper, because programming in SMALLTALK-80 means to use all the interactive facilities of a highly window-ori ented system. Nevertheless, we use our queue example to give an idea on how classes in SMALLTALK can be defined:

class name   Queue

instance variable names   waitingLine front rear items max

methods

    isEmpty
       ↑ items = 0

    isFull
       ↑ items = max

    insert: anElement
       self isFull
        ifTrue: [↑ false]
        ifFalse: [rear ← (rear rem max) + 1.
              waitingLine at: rear put: anElement.
              items ← items + 1.
              ↑ true]

      ...

    initialize: aSize
       items ← 0.
       front ← 1.
       max ← aSize.
       rear ← max.
       waitingLine ← Array new: (aSize + 1)

    new: aSize
       ↑ self new initialize: aSize

The method **new:** is used to instantiate a Queue: self new creates an uninitialized instance which receives the message **initialize** with the argument **aSize**; the ↑ returns explicitly the initialized instance. The messages at: and put: in

    waitingLine at: rear put: anElement.

represent

    waitingLine[rear] := anElement;

in PASCAL notation, for example.

Now, back to the question of inheritance in SMALLTALK. Classes in SMALLTALK can be organized in a hierarchy. A class can depend on another class, i.e. it can be described as an extension of another class, which is called the corresponding *superclass*. A class that modifies or extends a class is said to be the *subclass* of that class. Subclasses *inherit* all instance variables and methods from the corresponding superclass. The inheritance concept is the same as described by the prefixing of classes in SIMULA 67 (cf Section 7.4).

A subclass can add instance variables and methods to the inherited ones. While the names of added instance variables must differ from the inherited ones, the names of methods can be the same. In this case, a method of a superclass is overridden by a method of the subclass having the same name. However, the usage of the pseudo-variable `super` allows the overridden method to be used, i.e. `super` invokes the appropriate method from the superclass for a received message. (A pseudo-variable is available in every method. It must not be explicitly declared, and its value cannot be changed by assignment. Important pseudo-variable names are `nil`, `true`, and `false`.)

Everything in SMALLTALK is an object [HORO 84] and every object is an instance of a class (this is a profound difference to SIMULA 67). The SMALLTALK-80 system knows one top-class which is not a subclass of another class and which is called `Object`. Classes which a programmer creates are always subclasses of other classes (at least of the class `Object`), i.e. a superclass - subclass relationship must be given. Now, when defining a class on the basis of an existing one, the newly defined class inherits the properties of the corresponding superclass, as well as the properties of the superclass's superclass, and so on. Our above defined class `Queue` is at least a subclass of class `Object` and inherits methods from this class. The sequence of classes which are ancestors for a given class define an *inheritance chain* ending in the class `Object`. When an object receives a message it is first tried to find a method to respond to this message in the object's class. If no method is found, the inheritance chain is backtracked, i.e. the class's superclass is sought for a matching method, and so forth. Again, we consider the example given at the end of the preceding Section to explain inheritance in SMALLTALK:

```
class name                    C1
instance variable names
methods
    alpha
        self  beta
    beta
        printString 'beta in C1'
```

class name   C2
superclass   C1
instance variable names
methods
    beta
        printString 'beta in C2'

Now, assume that object x is an instantiation of class C1, and object y is an instantiation of class C2. Sending message alpha to x invokes method alpha of class C1 which sends message beta to self. Class C1 can respond to message beta by invoking method beta. Thus, the output is 'beta in C1', which is the same when sending message beta to x. Sending message beta to y invokes method beta in class C2 and, therefore, the output is 'beta in C2'. Sending message alpha to y is again the interesting point. Class C2 cannot respond to message alpha, thus, alpha is sought in the superclass C1. Method alpha of class C1 is invoked, and alpha sends message beta to self, which is now y. Thus, it is verified whether class C2 can respond to message beta. It can, since class C2 contains a method with name beta. This means, method beta of class C2 is invoked and the output is 'beta in C2'.

One major aspect of inheritance is to have code only at a single place in the system and, thus, reusing that code. Therefore, it is of great importance for a programmer to know exactly what code can be find in the class hierarchy. This is probably the greatest problem with the SMALLTALK-80 system – to know about all the code in the class hierarchy, which is provided by the system.

The inheritance concept in SMALLTALK is also discussed in [SETH 89] where different examples are considered.

7.6 Inheritance in C++

As for SIMULA 67, classes in C++ represent not only an encapsulation facility, but also an inheritance facility. Again, this means that this Section is closely related to Chapter 6 where we introduced the basic ideas of C++ classes, as well as the basic syntactical structures needed to declare and use them.

The overall concept is the same as already introduced for SIMULA 67 or SMALLTALK: classes can be defined on the basis of another class, i.e. they can be an extension of an existing class, thus supporting reusibility and extendibility [SMIT 90]. In C++ terminology we talk about *derived classes* instead of subclasses, and *base classes* instead of superclasses. Derived classes *inherit* the properties (i.e. the variables and operations) of the corresponding base classes; additionally they contain their own specific properties.

Recall the principle form of a class declaration:

```
class   name   {
      members
   public:
      members
}
```

where public members are visible outside, and others (the private ones) are not. Now the principle form of a derived class is as follows:

```
class   derived name : base name   {
      added members
}
```

An important question is now the visibility of inherited members. The default of the above given construct is that members inherited from the base class are private to the derived class, no matter whether they have been public or not in the base class. This means, that the members of the derived class can use the inherited members, but the inherited members are not accessible to users of the derived class. If this is desired, the base class has to be declared public:

```
class   derived name : public base name   {
      added members
}
```

This means, that a public member of the base class is also a public member of the derived class and, thus, can be accessed by the users of the derived class. Of course, private members of a base class remain private in the derived class, they cannot be made public in the derived class.

We conclude this Section by considering again the example of the two classes C1 and C2, which is given as a C++ fragment as follows:

```
class   C1 {
   public:
      void   alpha ();
      void   beta ();
};
      ...

void   C1::alpha () {
          this -> beta();
};
```

```
void  C2::beta ()  {
        cout << "beta in C1";
};

      ...

class  C2  :  public  C1  {
  public:
      void  beta ();
};

      ...

void  C2::beta () {
        cout << "beta in C2";
};

      ...

main ()  {
      C1  x;
      C2  y;

      ...

      x.alpha();      x.beta();
      y.alpha();      y.beta();
}
```

With x.alpha() we invoke function alpha of class C1, which itself invokes function beta of class C1. The result is the same as with x.beta: the output is "beta in C1". With y.beta() we invoke function beta of class C2, and the output is "beta in C2". Again, y.alpha() is the interesting point. y.alpha() invokes alpha of C1, which was bound to beta of C1 at compile time. Therefore, alpha invokes beta of C1, and the output is "beta in C1". This is quite different to SMALLTALK-80, and we see that inheritance works different in different languages.

However, it is possible to gain the same result as in SMALLTALK-80 by declaring beta() in class C1 to be a *virtual function*, as follows

```
class  C1 {
  public:
      void  alpha ();
      virtual void  beta ();
};
```

This means, that whenever possible beta() of the derived class will be invoked and, thus, the output for our example would be "beta in C2".

8 Concurrency

As already mentioned in Chapter 4, we call any program unit that can be in concurrent execution with other program units a task. In Chapter 4 we introduced coroutines and tasks in terms of unit control structures. The purpose of this Chapter is to have a closer look at concurrent program units, the basic ideas underlaying concurrency, and features in programming languages which are necessary to support concurrency. An overview of the developments in concurrency and communication as they took place during the last years is given in [HOAR 90].

After discussing the basic ideas we introduce coroutines in SIMULA 67 as an example of quasi-parallelism. Thereafter, we consider concurrent units which are used to satisfy a common goal. Such units need to *communicate* to each other and they need to be *synchronized*. Thus, we will discuss appropriate methods: Shared variables, semaphores, monitors, and messages. The Chapter is concluded by an example of concurrency in ADA.

8.1 Basic Ideas

When talking about the execution of programs on a computer system, we can distinguish between the two fundamental concepts

- *sequential execution*, and

- *concurrent execution*.

Sequential execution means that one statement after the other is executed and, thus, at any given time only one statement is in execution. In contrast to this, concurrency stands for parallel execution – or at least the possibility of parallelism. We call statement sequences, that can be executed in parallel, *processes*.

Obviously, things can only be done in parallel on a machine, if there are facilities available allowing parallelism. Real parallelism cannot be achieved without an appropriate hardware, i.e. without a computer system consisting of several processors. In this case we talk about a *multiprocessor* system providing physical parallelism. The operating systems of today's single processor computer systems usually allow a form of *quasi-parallelism* which is called *multiprogramming*. This means, that on such a system only one process is active at a time, but each process gets access to the processor for a certain time slice, and there exists a sophisticated scheduling algorithm to manage the demands of the different processes. For a more detailed discussion on such operating system facilities see [SILB 88], for example.

Now, the important issue for our discussion is that concurrency in programming languages and parallelism in computer systems are two different things. Concurrency in a programming language can be understood as parallelism on a logical level, i.e. the programming language provides facilities to specify which parts of a program (or a system in general) could be executed in parallel. Parallelism in computer systems stands for multiprocessor systems, or at least multiprogramming systems. So far it is not important for our considerations, whether the underlaying hardware system actually allows physical parallelism, or just a form of quasi-parallelism. We are interested in the features, which programming languages must provide to allow concurrency.

But why do we need concurrency at all? Because various real life problems are existing, which can (or must) be modelled by concurrent program units. For example, every system consisting of a process (or several processes) producing some entities which are consumed by another process (or processes) can be modelled in a natural way using concurrent units. In general, the requirement for concurrency can be found in

- *simulations* of real life situations consisting of several parallel activities interacting with each other, such as flow of information in an office environment, or traffic situations representing an airport (i.e. simulations of producer-consumer problems);

- *actual systems* to manage parallel activities (i.e. producer-consumer situations), such as process control systems (e.g. for a power plant), or computer operating systems;

- approaches to *improve efficiency* when performing the calculations for a certain problem by doing appropriate calculations in parallel. Obviously, efficiency improvements can only be achieved, if the logical parallelism can be mapped onto physical parallelism. This issue becomes more and more important, since multiprocessor systems become now available.

Processes or concurrent units are typically not totally independent of each other, rather they interact in certain ways. The two forms of interaction are

- *communication*, and

- *synchronization*.

Synchronization means controlling the order of execution of processes. This becomes necessary either if the processes *compete* for the same resources, or if they *cooperate* to perform a common goal. In any case, the processes have to communicate for this reason.

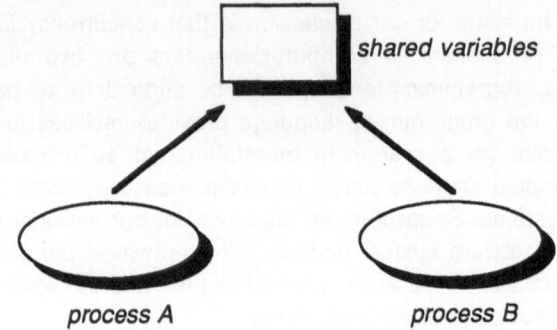

a) information exchange using shared variables

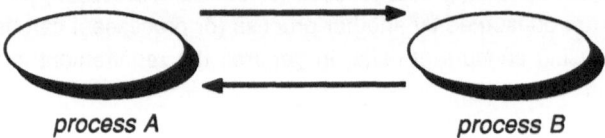

b) information exchange using messages

Fig. 8.1.   Forms of process communication

Communication, i.e. the exchange of information or data, between processes can take place either by sending *messages* or simply by using common memory, i.e. to have *shared variables* (cf Figure 8.1). Obviously, the usage of shared variables can cause some problems. We have to ensure that a process does not access variables which are currently updated by another process. Therefore, we need some locking mechanisms which prevent the simultaneous access to variables (i.e. which guarantee mutually exclusive access to shared data).

Those problems are subject of the following Sections. But we start with an example of quasi-parallelism: Coroutines in SIMULA 67.

8.2   Coroutines in SIMULA 67

Recall that coroutines allow the simulation of interleaved processes. The above mentioned simulations of producer-consumer paradigms can be handled using coroutines (e.g. the simulation of a single server system, as shown in Chapter 4, where the queue process is the producer and the server process represents the consumer). Coroutines are a form of procedures allowing the mutual activation of each other in an explicit way. The activation of a coroutine A by a coroutine B means that the execution of coroutine B is suspended, while the execution of coroutine A is resumed at that point where it has been suspended last. The situation is the same as for procedures: At any given time there is only one coroutine in execution.

Coroutines in SIMULA 67 are realized by *classes* and the primitives RESUME and DETACH. The general form of a coroutine in SIMULA 67 could be given as follows:

```
CLASS P;
BEGIN
     initialization statements
     DETACH;
     WHILE   TRUE   DO
     BEGIN
          process statements
          RESUME  (…);
     END;
END;
```

Assume the pointer variable

```
REF (P) p1;
```

which is instantiated by executing

```
p1 :- NEW P;
```

On executing this statement a new class object is instantiated, i.e. a new incarnation of class P is created and the class body is started to be executed. The execution of DETACH suspends the execution of the coroutine and control is returned to that unit (the master) which created the incarnation of the class (i.e. execution is continued with the statement next to p1 :- NEW P;). Thus, DETACH is normally used to allow some initializations before starting the actual simulation.

The semantics of the RESUME primitive can best be compared with a procedure call mechanism. RESUME(x) transfers control to coroutine x. The difference to a procedure call is that execution does not start with the first statement of the class body, but with that statement following the statement which was last executed (e.g. with WHILE TRUE DO … if DETACH was the last executed statement).

Thus, SIMULA 67 provides explicit control mechanisms with the primitives RESUME and DETACH, and the programmer has to decide when control should be transfered to another coroutine. This means, we have an explicit form of mutual activation, and these primitives are used for synchronization. Communication between coroutines can take place either by using shared variables (i.e. global variables) or by referencing variables of other coroutines.

The following simple example should give an impression on how a producer-consumer problem can be simulated using the facilities provided by SIMULA 67. To simplify matters, we assume that the producer process (represented by the class prod) just produces random numbers in the interval [1, 50] using the build-in function RANDINT. The consumer process (represented by class cons) consumes these random numbers in a way that is not specified in detail.

```
BEGIN

COMMENT ** implementation of producer-consumer processes;
COMMENT ** Author: B. Teufel

    BOOLEAN over;
        COMMENT ** controls the life of the processes;
    INTEGER number;
        COMMENT ** the shared variable;

COMMENT ** the producer;

CLASS prod;
BEGIN
    REF (cons) cref;
    INTEGER u;
    u := ININT;
    DETACH;
    WHILE  NOT over  DO
    BEGIN
        number := RANDINT(1,50,u);
        RESUME(cref);
    END;
END;
```

```
COMMENT ** the consumer;

CLASS cons;
BEGIN
      REF (prod) pref;
      INTEGER i, j;
      i := ININT;
      DETACH;
      WHILE  NOT over  DO
      BEGIN
            j := number;
            IF  i = j  THEN

                ...

            ELSE

                ...

            RESUME (pref);
      END;
END;

COMMENT ** the master;

REF (prod) p1;
REF (cons) c1;

over := FALSE;
p1 :- NEW prod;
c1 :- NEW cons;
p1.cref :- c1;
c1.pref :- p1;
RESUME (p1);
END;
```

The produced entities, i.e. the random integer numbers, of coroutine p1 are transfered to coroutine c1 using the global variable number. The initialization parts of both coroutines (given before the DETACH statement) just read in integer numbers to initialize the variables u and i, respectively.

The master unit instantiates the reference variables p1 and c1, i.e. it creates the corresponding coroutines. The reference variable of the consumer and producer process is connected to the incarnation of each other's process, respectively. Then, the master unit starts the producer-consumer process with RESUME (p1). Thus, it is ensured that the shared variable number contains a value before this value is consumed by c1. The usage of the RESUME statements describes the synchronization of the two coroutines.

We can assume that the control variable over is set in the consumer coroutine. When it is set to true, the execution of the coroutine instance terminates and control is transfered back to the program unit that activated the coroutines, i.e. the master units.

The implementation of coroutines is similar to the implementation of procedures. Like procedures, coroutines are represented by activation records. The major difference is that on the exit of a procedure, this procedure is terminated and, therefore, the corresponding activation record can be popped off the stack. When exiting a coroutine, the current status of the coroutine must be saved as well as a pointer to the statement where the execution continues on the next resume of the coroutine. The corresponding activation record cannot be popped off the stack. This leads to the requirement that each coroutine has its own activation record stack.

8.3   Semaphores

In the previous Section we have shown that communication between coroutines via shared variables makes no difficulties, because there is only one coroutine active at any time. Coroutines activate explicitly each other, and in doing so suspend themselves from execution. The introduced producer-consumer problems represent the concept of cooperation. The interaction between concurrent processes needs a bit more attention in terms of synchronization for cooperation (producer-consumer problems) as well as competition (accessing shared data structures).

The competition problem can be explained by the following example. Suppose a self-service filling station where A fills up his car. When finished, A first goes to the snack bar having a cup of coffee instead of directly going to the cashier and paying. In the meantime B arrives at the filling station, also filling up his car. Since there was no reset of the meter and the petrol pump was not locked, B's consumption is added to that of A. When B has finished, A goes to the cashier. Since A believes that computerized systems are without fail, he pays not only his coffee, but also his and B's fuel (of course a bit astonished at the total amount). B is lucky, because the meter is already reset to zero when he is going to pay.

Thus, the problems are imaginable when two processes compete for the same entities. We need to have some form of synchronization when accessing shared data structures, i.e. we must avoid that a process has access to a shared variable or data structure, while another process is manipulating that structure. Dijkstra describes this situation as follows [DIJK 68b]: "... *the indivisible accesses to common variables are always 'one-way information traffic': an individual process can either assign a new value or inspect a current value. Such an inspection itself, however, leaves no trace for the other processes, and the consequence is that, when a process wants to react to the current value of a common variable, that variable's value may have been changed by the other processes between the moment of its inspection and the following effectuation of the reaction to it."*

Dijkstra introduced the semaphore concept as a method allowing such a synchronization [DIJK 68a], [DIJK 68b]. The semaphore concept is represented by "*special-purpose integers*", the *semaphores*, and two primitives, the *P-operation* and the *V-operation*. Both operations have a semaphore variable, say s, as an argument. While the function of the V-operation is to increase its argument by 1 (i.e. V(s) performs s := s + 1), the function of the P-operation is to wait until its argument is greater 0, and then to decrease its argument by 1 (i.e. P(s) delays until s > 0 and then performs s := s − 1). Both, the P-operation and the V-operation are executed as indivisible operations. Andrews and Schneider report in [ANDR 83] that Dijkstra and his group state that P stands for "*prolagen*", being a combination of the two Dutch words "*proberen*" and "*verlagen*", while V stands for the Dutch word "*verhogen*". In literature the P-operation is often called *wait*, while the V-operation is usually called *signal* (see [SEBE 89] or [HORO 84], for example).

Some terminology:

- *Processes* are concurrently executed sequences of statements.

- *Critical section* or *region* stands for a sequence of statements which accesses a shared variable or data structure and, therefore, must be executed indivisible.

- *Mutual exclusion* ensures that a sequence of statements (e.g. a critical section) is executed indivisible.

- *Fair scheduling* ensures that every process which is waiting (i.e. executing the P-operation) will enter the critical section in finite time, i.e. is not delayed forever (provided that any process, executing a critical section terminates this section in finite time, of course).

Now, the most interesting question is how to provide mutual exclusion of a critical section using semaphores. The answer is quite simple and in principle given by the following fragment, where we suppose to have to processes (p1 and p2) and a single semaphore variable (s) being used by both processes:

```
var  s  :  SEMAPHORE;
...
process p1;
   begin
          ...     (* the noncritical section *)
       P(s);
```

```
              …       (* the critical section      *)
          V(s);
              …       (* the noncritical section *)
       end;
    …
    process p2;
       begin
              …       (* the noncritical section *)
          P(s);
              …       (* the critical section      *)
          V(s);
              …       (* the noncritical section *)
       end;
```

This means, mutual exclusion of all critical sections can be ensured using the same semaphore and encapsulating the critical section by the P-operation and the V-operation. The interpretation of the code fragment is obvious: Whenever a process tries to enter a critical section, it first executes the P-operation using the semaphore s. This means the process waits until s is greater zero, indicating that the execution of the critical section can be allowed (i.e. no other process has access to the shared data structure, for example). Naturally, the semaphore s must be initialized by 1. An initialization of zero for the semaphore would create a deadlock, since the zero value for the semaphore indicates that some process has access to a critical section and all others have to wait until that process finishes the execution of the critical section. On termination of a critical section a process always executes the V-operation, i.e. s := s + 1, giving a signal to the other processes that one of them can now execute its own critical section. The overall situation is illustrated in Figure 8.2.

Thoroughly considering the above given description, we recognize that the semaphore itself is a shared variable, and that the operations on it are critical sections, i.e. they must be done mutually exclusive. This is achieved by implementing the operations using low-level test-and-set operations, which indivisibly test and assign a value.

It follows from our introduction that the value range of semaphores is given by 0 and 1 (or false and true). Thus, we find often the term binary semaphores. Semaphores that can take any positive value are called general semaphores and are usually used for resource allocation. Then, the semaphore is not initialized by 1, but by the number of units of a certain resource (e.g. the number of printers). The semantic of general semaphores is the same as for binary semaphores. A value of zero means that all resources are connected to a process and that processes demanding that resource must wait. Any positive number between zero and the initial value of the semaphore specifies the number of available resources. Those problems are of interest in operating systems, for instance.

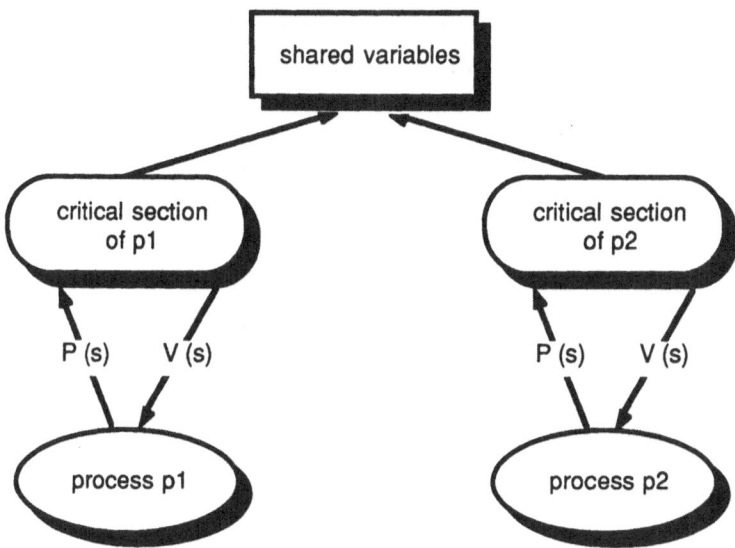

Fig. 8.2. Using semaphores to ensure mutual exclusion of critical sections

ALGOL 68 provides the type `sema` to declare semaphore variables, and the functions `up` and `down` representing the V-operation and P-operation, respectively. Concurrent program units in ALGOL 68 are specified as sequences of statements enclosed by `begin` and `end`, and separated by a comma. Statements or units which are separated by a comma are called *collateral statements*, and can be executed in parallel.

8.4   Monitors

Semaphores, as introduced in the preceding Section, represent one method to ensure mutual exclusion of critical sections, accessing shared variables. Monitors are another approach to perform mutual exclusion for the access of shared variables. The principle idea of monitors is strongly influenced by encapsulation concepts and abstract data types:

- Shared variables and operations on them are grouped together and encapsulated in a unit called *monitor*. The shared variables or data structures can only be accessed by the procedures which are provided by the monitor, and these procedures provide mutual exclusive access by scheduling the processes.

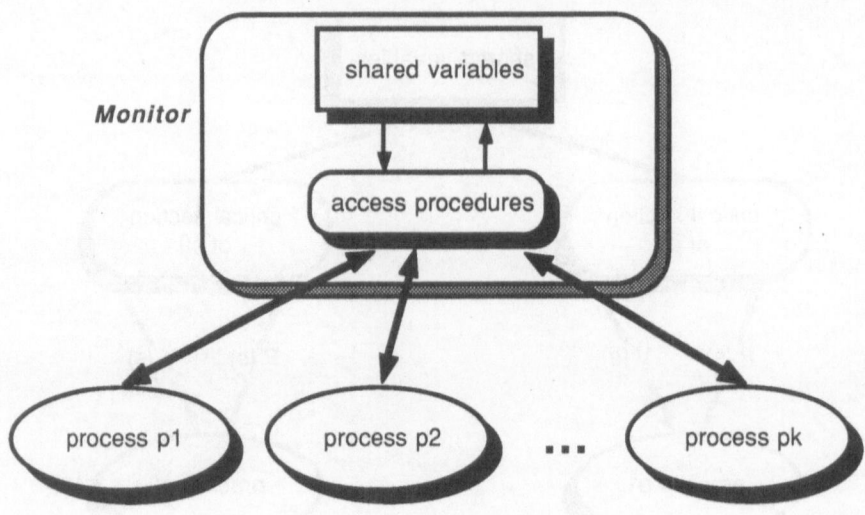

Fig. 8.3. The monitor concept

Like abstract data types for the manipulation of variables, monitors are an elegant and clearly structured way to provide synchronization for the access of shared variables. In both cases, the major actions are performed at one place in a system. Processes that want access to shared variables use the "exported" procedures, and their synchronization is done by the monitor itself using the semaphore concept (cf Figure 8.3). Contrary, the usage of semaphores in each process that has access to a shared variable means that every process has to use the P- and V-operations as brackets. Especially when considering a great number of processes, the synchronization using semaphores seems to be an unmethodological and chaotic approach with a high probability for errors, since synchronization is not concentrated to one place.

The monitor concept originates in works of Dijkstra, Brinch Hansen and Hoare [BRIN 73], [HOAR 74]. The first programming language providing the monitor concept was CONCURRENT PASCAL by Per Brinch Hansen. CONCURRENT PASCAL is "*an abstract programming language for structured programming of computer operating systems. It extends the sequential programming language PASCAL with concurrent processes, monitors, and classes*" [BRIN 75a]. MESA is another programming language which also provides monitors [MITC 79].

We choose CONCURRENT PASCAL to exemplify a programming language's facilities for concurrent programming and synchronization using the monitor concept. How to use CONCURRENT PASCAL is described in [BRIN 75b], for instance. According to the CONCURRENT PASCAL report [BRIN 75a] a concurrent program consists of three kinds of so-called system types: PROCESS, MONITOR, and CLASS. The general form of declaration is as follows:

> type   *name* = *system type* (*formal parameters*) ;   *block*

where *name* is the name of a process, monitor, or class, and *system type* is the appropriate type name. *block* stands for declarations and a compound statement, i.e. a sequence of statements encapsulated with a BEGIN END pair, and executed one at a time from left to right. The block or body of a monitor, for example, can contain private procedures and public procedures (declared to be public by using the keyword entry), as well as some initialization code. We quote from [BRIN 75a]:

- *A process type defines a data structure and a sequential statement that can operate on it.*

- *A monitor type defines a data structure and the operations that can be performed on it by concurrent processes. These operations can synchronize processes and exchange data among them.*

- *A class type defines a data structure and the operations on it by a single process or monitor. These operations provide controlled access to the data.*

Variables of a system type are called system components and are initialized by an init statement:

> init   *variable name* (*actual parameters*)

The semantics of such an init statement is that space for locally declared variables is allocated, and the initial statement is executed. Once an init statement is executed the parameters and the variables of the system component exist forever.

As already mentioned, synchronization for the controlled access of shared variables is done within the monitor and not by each process. Therefore, the language must provide some facilities to delay processes, in case they require access to a shared variable which is occupied by another process. These facilities in CONCURRENT PASCAL are a queue data type together with its two operations delay and continue on variables of that type. A queue variable, say q, is defined within a monitor, and when executing delay(q) by a certain process, that process is delayed in queue q. The semantics of the continue statement is, that the process executing continue(q) within a monitor routine returns from the monitor (i.e. the shared variables can be accessed by other processes), and if a process is waiting in q, that process is removed from q and resumes its execution of the appropriate monitor routine. Then, the resumed process is given exclusive access to the shared variables.

The standard type `queue` allows only *one* process to wait in a single queue at a time. But this is not a major restriction, since a multiprocess queue can simply be defined as an array of single process queues:

```
type  MultiQ  =  array (.0..qlngth-1.) of queue;
```

The principle form on how a producer-consumer problem can be specified using CONCURRENT PASCAL is given by the following program fragment, where we assume that the shared data structure is a FIFO-buffer with appropriate insert and remove procedures, as already explained for the examples for abstract data types in Chapter 6. A monitor is defined, specifying the shared data structure `buffer`, and two procedures to manipulate the FIFO-buffer, which are declared to be entry procedures, i.e. they can be used by other processes. Both, the producer and consumer are declared as a process type, consisting of a `cycle` statement. A `cycle` statement defines a sequence of statements to be executed repeatedly forever.

```
const  max = 100;

type  FB  =  monitor
             var  buffer : array (.1..max.) of integer;
                  items  : integer;
                  front  : integer;
                  rear   : integer;
                  send   : queue;
                  rec    : queue;

             procedure entry insert (el: integer);
             begin
                  if  items = max  then  delay(send);
                  rear := (rear mod max) + 1;
                  buffer(.rear.) := el;
                  items := items + 1;
                  continue(rec);
             end;

             procedure entry remove (VAR el: element);
             begin
                  if  items = 0  then  delay(rec);
                  el := buffer(.front.);
                  front := (front mod max) + 1;
                  items := items - 1;
                  continue(send);
             end;
```

```
begin       (* monitor initialization *)
   items := 0;
   front := 1;
   rear  := max;
end;

Cons = process (buf: FB)
         var  el  :  integer;
       begin
         cycle

            ...

            buf.remove(el);

            ...

         end
       end;

Prod = process (buf: FB)
         var  el  :  integer;
       begin
         cycle

            ...

            buf.insert(el);

            ...

         end
       end;

var  p  :  Prod;
     c  :  Cons;
     b  :  FB;

begin
     init  b,  p(b),  c(b)
end;
```

The synchronization of the producer and consumer process is done by the monitor using the queues send and rec. The producer process is delayed, if the buffer is full, i.e. an overflow of the buffer is avoided by executing delay(send), and it is resumed by the consumer process executing continue(send). In the same way an underflow of the buffer is avoided by executing delay(rec), i.e. the consumer process is delayed. The consumer process is resumed by the producer by executing continue(rec). The declared system components p, c, and b are instantiated by the init statement, which creates the shared data structure and starts the execution of the producer and consumer processes.

8.5 Messages

Semaphores and monitors describe good approaches to synchronize communication between concurrent processes on the basis of shared data structures. Therefore, both methods are good solutions for quasi-parallel implementations on multi-programmed single-processor systems. Here, we actually do find the situation of shared memory.

Considering multiprocessor systems (allowing physical parallelism) we might find the situation that each processor has its own (private) memory and, therefore, communication between processes executed on those processors cannot be done by shared data structures, but must be done in a somehow natural way of communication: Processes send and wait for *messages*. This means that, as a basic requirement, some form of a communication channel must be established, and that programming languages must provide message send and wait (or receive) features to allow the synchronization of processes. Communication between two processes by means of messages means that both processes must demonstrate their willingness to communicate, i.e. both must reach a certain point in their execution, where they need to exchange information. Delaying that process, which reaches this point first, until the other process also reaches his communication point, means synchronising the processes.

Like monitors, the message passing model is based on research done by Brinch Hansen [BRIN 78] and Hoare [HOAR 78]. Both provide a language concept for the communication of concurrent processes without having shared variables, and both apply Dijkstra's ideas of guarded commands [DIJK 75] to handle the nondeterministic nature of concurrent processes. Brinch Hansen's concept for concurrent programming is called *distributed processes*, while that of Hoare is called *communicating sequential processes* (CSP).

Both approaches, distributed processes and communicating sequential processes, consider the process as the fundamental issue, which can be in concurrent execution. In general, processes have a declaration part, defining local entities, and command or statement sequences. Processes communicate by sending messages to each other. Brinch Hansen introduces the following syntax for such a communication between a process P and a process Q:

```
call Q.R (expr, var)
```

which is based on a procedure call mechanism, i.e. this command in process P causes the call of procedure R in process Q. Procedures are simply given in the form

```
proc   name (input # output)
        declarations
        statements
```

Calling procedure R means that the values of `expr` are assigned to the formal parameters of R, describing the input. On termination of R the output is assigned to `var`. Thus, the communication between the processes P and Q become obvious: P sends certain values to Q as input parameters for procedure R, and Q returns the output values of procedure R to P. This procedural communication concept is reflected in the fact that the calling process has to wait until the called procedure terminates, i.e. "...*the process is idle until the other process has completed the operation* (i.e. the procedure) *requested by it*" [BRIN 78].

Brinch Hansen distinguishes between guarded commands and guarded regions to control nondeterminism. Recall, guarded commands given as

```
guard    →    statement-list
```

(where `guard` is a boolean expression) were introduced by Dijkstra as a building block for selections and repetitions, allowing nondeterministic program components. Thus, in *distributed processes* a guarded command of the form

```
if  B1 : S1  |  B2 : S2  |  …  end
```

enables a process to make an arbitrary choice among those conditions `Bi` which are true, and execute the corresponding statement `Si`. If none of the conditions is true, the process is stopped. *Guarded regions* differ in that they enable a process to wait until the state of its variables allows an arbitrary choice among several statements, i.e. the process is not stopped, although no alternative can be chosen. The syntactical forms of guarded regions are given as

```
when   B1 : S1  |  B2 : S2  |  …  end
cycle  B1 : S1  |  B2 : S2  |  …  end
```

where the first causes a process to wait until one of the conditions becomes true, and, then, to execute the appropriate statement. The `cycle` statement just stands for an endless repetition of a `when` statement.

Hoare introduced a slightly different form for the communication between two processes. Communication between two processes in CSP is specified by input and output commands, the syntax of which is as follows:

```
input command    →    source  ?  target variable
output command   →    destination  !  expression
source           →    process name
destination      →    process name
```

Thus, an input command in a process Q, such as

```
P ? a
```

expresses an input request of Q from P, resulting in the assignment of an input value to variable a, which is local to Q. The input command may be executed only when P is ready to execute a corresponding output command:

```
Q ! b
```

meaning to export the value of variable b, which is local to P, to process Q. Analogously to Brinch Hansen's distributed processes, CSP processes have to wait for another process to be ready to receive a communication. Different in CSP is that when both processes are synchronized, execution of the processes continues simultaneously.

According to Hoare [HOAR 78], input and output commands correspond when an input command in process A specifies as its source process B, and an output command in process B specifies as its destination process A, and when the target variable of A's input command matches the value denoted by the expression of B's output command. In this case communication between A and B is possible. As in Brinch Hansen's distributed processes, nondeterminism is controlled in CSP using Dijkstra's guarded commands (with a slight change of notation).

A simple example (the classical bounded buffer example) should give an overview of CSP. For this reason, we consider again a producer-consumer process, communicating via a buffer-process, which manages a buffer (buf) of size 10. The producer process produces elements for the buffer, while the consumer process consumes the elements from the buffer. The buffer-process synchronizes the producer and consumer process and is given as follows:

```
buffer::
buf: (1..10) element;

front, rear, items: integer;
front := 1;
rear := 1;
items := 0;
```

```
*[ items < 10; producer ? buf(rear)   →
       items := items + 1;
       rear := (rear mod 10) + 1;
    ‖  items > 0; consumer ? more()   →
       consumer ! buf(front);
       front := (front mod 10) + 1;
       items := items - 1;
 ]
```

The buffer-process requests input from the producer-process by

```
producer ? buf(rear)
```

which, of course, must contain the matching output command

```
buffer ! el
```

The communication with the consumer-process is done in a bit more complicated form, i.e. the consumer-process is requested for a signal indicating that it is ready:

```
consumer ? more()
```

(more() acts just as a signal). The actual transfer of elements is done by

```
consumer ! buf(front)
```

The consumer-process consists of the two matching commands

```
buffer ! more()
buffer ? el
```

The construct * [...] is a repetitive alternative command, consisting of two guarded commands in our example. The guards are given as

```
items < 10; producer ? buf(rear)
items > 0; consumer ? more()
```

and are separated by the guard separator ‖. Important is that guards can consist of boolean conditions and/or input commands. A command list which is connected to a guard can only be executed if the guard does not fail, i.e. if the boolean expression is true, and if the input command is synchronized with appropriate output command.

8.6   Concurrency in ADA

In ADA, a concurrent process is called *task*. A task is described similarly to a package in ADA: it consists of a specification and a task body. Thus, the general form is as follows:

```
task  T  is
    -- task specification
    -- describing the interface to other tasks

    ...
end;

task body  T  is
    -- task body
    -- describing the task's dynamic behaviour

    ...
end;
```

As for packages, the task specification and its body share the same name.

ADA's concept of interaction between tasks was strongly influenced by the above introduced concepts of message passing. In ADA the mechanism allowing the communication between tasks is called *rendezvous*, which means nothing else than in every day life, when two people meet to perform a certain action, and then continue independently.

A task specification describes so-called *entry* points, showing other tasks where and in which way it allows communication. An entry is defined and called similarly to a procedure (especially it can - but must not – have in, in out, and out parameters). An entry's parameters describe the exchange of information between tasks. Its general form is given as

```
entry  name (formal parameters);
```

An entry declared in a specification of a task has to have its corresponding implementation in the task body – similar to procedures having their declaration in the package specification and their implementation in the package body. For this reason ADA provides the so-called *accept* clause which has the form

```
accept  name (formal parameters)  do
    -- statement sequence
end;
```

where the name in the accept clause matches the name in the entry clause. As already mentioned the parameters describe the communication between the task calling the entry and that task executing the corresponding accept clause. The parameter mechanism itself is the same as for procedure calls. Omitting the parameters has the one and only purpose of synchronising two tasks, as it might be necessary in some exceptional cases (such as to give the signal to open a valve in case of overpressure in a pressure system).

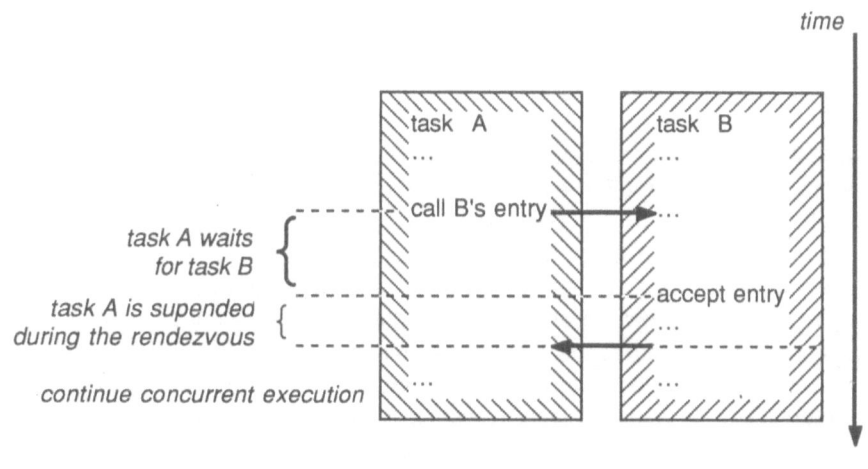

a) task A waits for task B

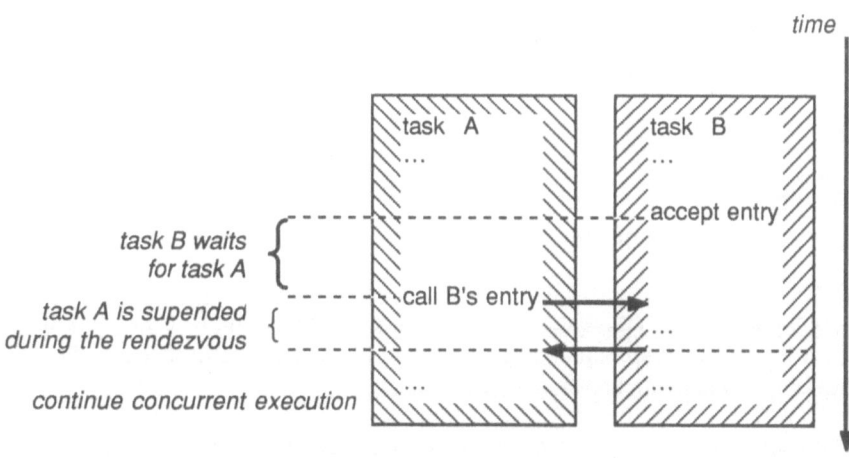

b) task B waits for task A

Fig. 8.4. The rendezvous concept

The statement sequence of the accept clause describes the actions to be performed during the rendezvous between two tasks. Obviously, this statement sequence can also be the empty set which, again, just indicates a synchronization between two tasks. The statements of an accept clause can consist of blocks, procedure calls, entry calls as well as other accept statements. Obviously, further accept statements can only be given for different entries to keep unambiguous.

As usual, a rendezvous can take place between two tasks, say A and B, only if both tasks are ready to communicate, i.e. if, for example, A executes an entry call of B and, if B is ready to execute the corresponding accept statement. If this is not fulfilled, one of the tasks, either A or B, has to wait for the other task. This situation is shown in Figure 8.4.

Figure 8.4a shows the situation where A executes an entry call of B while B is still busy to perform some other actions. This means A has to wait until B reaches its accept statement (i.e. A is enqueued in a waiting line for B). Figure 8.4b shows the situation where task B is ready to communicate, i.e. it reached already its accept statement, but task A is still busy. Thus in this case, B has to wait until A reaches the corresponding entry call. In any case, the task calling an entry of another task is suspended during the rendezvous takes place. The termination of the accept clause indicates that both tasks can continue independently and simultaneously. An interesting difference to Hoare's communicating sequential processes is that only the calling task has to know the name of the other task (recall, that both primitives "!", and "?" require a task name).

ADA introduces nondeterminism by a select statement of the form

```
select
     select alternative
or
     select alternative
...
else
     statement sequence
end select;
```

where the select alternative can contain an accept statement. Now nondeterminism means that if all accept statements have non-empty queues of tasks waiting for a rendezvous, one is chosen nondeterministically.

The accept statements can be combined with guards of the form

```
when   boolean expression   =>   ...
```

Doing this in a select statement, each time the select statement is reached, all the guards are evaluated and only those accept statements are considered for a rendezvous, where the guards are true.

To give an impression on how these language features can be used, we show an ADA implementation of the bounded buffer problem:

```
task   BUFFER   is
       entry INSERT (EL: in ELEMENT);
       entry REMOVE (EL: out ELEMENT);
end;

task body  BUFFER  is
       BUF : array (1..10) of ELEMENT;
       FRONT, REAR : INTEGER 1..10 := 1;
       ITEMS : INTEGER 0..10 := 0;

       begin
          loop
             select
                when  ITEMS < 10  =>
                   accept   INSERT (EL: in ELEMENT)   do
                      BUF(REAR) := EL;
                   end;
                   REAR := (REAR mod 10) + 1;
                   ITEMS := ITEMS + 1;
             or
                when  ITEMS > 0  =>
                   accept  REMOVE (EL: out ELEMENT)   do
                      EL := BUF(FRONT);
                   end;
                   FRONT := (FRONT mod 10) + 1;
                   ITEMS := ITEMS - 1;
             end select;
          end loop;
       end;
```

Again, we have a pair of producer-consumer processes using this BUFFER task. The producer process contains a call

```
BUFFER.INSERT(EL1);
```

while the consumer process contains the call

```
BUFFER.REMOVE(EL1);
```

In the given example the guard controls the buffer to avoid an overflow or under-flow of the buffer, i.e. that the producer process cannot insert an element into a full buffer, and the consumer process cannot remove an element from an empty buffer.

Tasking in ADA is much more complex than it can be discussed within the scope of this book. Therefore, for more details we refer to [BARN 89].

9 Semantics

In Chapter one, the basic notations to describe the syntax of a programming language have been introduced. Since a programming language is a formal language with a relatively small number of rules describing its form (the syntax), it is not very difficult to find a formalism which allows to describe the syntax of the language. Such a description is given by BNF or syntax diagrams, for example. Describing the form of language constructs is much easier than describing their meaning – we are faced with similar problems as when considering one of Picasso's paintings, for example.

Much research work has been done to find a concise, unambiguous and readable notation to describe the semantics of a programming language. Unfortunately, as yet none of the proposals made has become a commonly agreed method to describe semantics. Therefore, natural language is still this medium which is mainly used to describe the semantics of a programming language. The problems with natural language are obvious: Natural language is somehow ambiguous and inexact and, thus, is interpreted in different ways by different people (e.g. the compiler writer and the user of the language).

Anyway, we want to introduce briefly the three major approaches in the description of semantics in programming languages. These approaches are: Operational semantics, denotational semantics, and axiomatic semantics. The first method introduces a virtual computer to describe the meaning of basic language concepts, while the others represent a mathematical way of description.

9.1   Why Formal Semantics?

In the above given introduction we already gave an idea, why it is necessary to have a concise description of the meaning of a programming language. Ambiguous and inconsistent descriptions are interpreted differently by different people.

According to the summery given in [GHEZ 82], the most important benefits of formal semantics are:

- Unambiguous semantics definition.

- Essential to compare language features.

- Independence from implementation.

- Basis to proof the correctness of the language implementation, as well as to proof the correctness of programs written in a certain language.

Using a simple formalism based on mathematical concepts allows an unambiguous definition of semantics. Such a formalism is represented by a meta-language, similar to the BNF notation, for instance. A meta-language permits to compare certain features of the same or of different languages on a precise foundation. Thus, language evaluations can be based on syntax and semantics without restrictions. Probably the most important advantage of a formal description of semantics is that we do not have to cope with specific details of an implementation, or with specific facilities of a (virtual) system.

Different interpretations of ambiguous descriptions have already been mentioned. Obviously, ambiguity cannot be the basis for proofing the correctness of an implementation. For this we need concise formal, i.e. mathematical, methods to describe not only the syntactical features of a programming language but, most of all, its semantic features.

9.2   Operational Semantics

Operational semantics is that approach which uses a virtual computer to describe the semantics of a programming language. Usually a simple abstract computer system is defined using an automaton model. Then, the basic idea is to describe the meaning of a program (representing the features of a certain language) by executing its statements on that abstract computer.

An abstract machine consists of some states and a set of simple instructions. The machine is defined by specifying how the machine changes its state by executing each of the instructions (i.e. describing a simple automaton model). Then, the semantics of the considered programming language is defined in terms of this abstract (or virtual) computer.

Important for this approach is that the resulting abstract machine is as simple as possible. It does not matter whether the defined machine can practically be used or not. What counts is that different interpretations of its code are not possible because of its simplicity. Similar to semantic analysis of a compiler which performs a translation of a source code into some intermediary code (cf Chapter 2), the semantic description of a programming language specifies a translation into the code of the abstract machine. The execution of machine instructions on that virtual computer causes some state transitions which describe the semantics of the corresponding programming language.

Unfortunately, actual approaches for operational semantics, such as the Vienna Definition Language, have shown that the operational method needs to take a lot of details into consideration. Thus, the desired simplicity of the operational approach cannot be achieved for real applications, rather the example of the Vienna Definition Language shows that operational semantics can result in a quite complex method.

The *Vienna Definition Language* (VDL) describes an operational approach to define the semantics of a programming language (see [WEGN 72]). VDL was introduced to describe the semantics of PL/1, but was not intensively used for other programming languages because of its complexity. Analogically to the above introduced operational approach, the semantics of a programming language is defined in VDL in terms of *state transitions* to which its programs give rise during execution. Every computation starts in an initial state and is represented by a sequence of state transitions. A transition takes place whenever a primitive instruction is executed.

9.3   Denotational Semantics

Denotational semantics is a formal (i.e. a logical and mathematical) method for defining the semantics of programming languages. It originates from the research done by Scott and Strachey [SCOT 70], [SCOT 71].

The method of denotational semantics is given in λ-notation which is based on the λ-calculus of Church [CHUR 41]. The λ-calculus is a notation for defining functions. The expressions of the notation are called λ-expressions, and each λ-expression denotes a function. Now, the denotational approach is to define programs in terms of (recursive) functions, i.e. a program *denotes* a function. Thus, the denotational semantics of a certain programming language describe the mapping from programs written in that language to the functions they denote. A function which is described by a program is composed by other functions representing individual program constructs.

A fairly good introduction to denotational semantics is given in [ALLI 86]. The method of denotational semantics of programming languages is rather complex and, thus, is beyond the scope of this book. But we want to introduce the classic example of decimal numerals to illustrate the method of denotational semantics.

The syntax of non-negative numbers of a programming language, say PL, could be described by the following simple grammar G (T, N, P, S):

```
T   =   { 0, 1, 2, 3, 4, 5, 6, 7, 8, 9 }
N   =   { DIGIT, NN }
P   =   { NN  →  DIGIT  |  NN  DIGIT  .
          DIGIT → 0 | 1 | 2 | 3 | 4 | 5 | 6 | 7 | 8 | 9  . }
S   =   { NN }
```

where T, the set of terminal symbols, describes the alphabet over which non-negative numbers can be generated; N denotes the set of non-terminals; P denotes the set of productions; S denotes the start symbol (cf Chapter 2). Thus, a non-negative number is either a digit, or a non-negative number followed by a digit. A digit is either a 0, or a 1, or a 2, and so forth, up to 9.

Usually, the non-negative numbers that can be created by the above given grammar denote non-negative integer objects. Therefore, we have to establish a function which represents the appropriate semantic values of such non-negative numbers, i.e. a semantic valuation function Φ that maps the abstract syntactic rules to the integer objects which they denote (using the conventional interpretation of such numbers). The function can be given in the following way:

Φ: PL → INTEGER

$\Phi\, [\![NN\ \ DIGIT]\!] = 10\, {}^{*}\, \Phi\, [\![NN]\!] + \Phi\, [\![DIGIT]\!]$

$\Phi\ [\![0]\!] = 0$	$\Phi\ [\![1]\!] = 1$
$\Phi\ [\![2]\!] = 2$	$\Phi\ [\![3]\!] = 3$
$\Phi\ [\![4]\!] = 4$	$\Phi\ [\![5]\!] = 5$
$\Phi\ [\![6]\!] = 6$	$\Phi\ [\![7]\!] = 7$
$\Phi\ [\![8]\!] = 8$	$\Phi\ [\![9]\!] = 9$

where the outlined square brackets enclose syntactic operands, i.e. elements of the vocabulary ($V^{*} = (T \cup N)^{*}$) of the language PL. It must be noted that, for example, a 4 between the outlined square brackets is an element of the alphabet which denotes the integer 4. This means, we find on the right hand side of the equal signs abstract integer objects which represent the semantic values of the elements between the outlined square brackets on the left hand side of the equal signs. Φ describes a mapping from T^{*}, i.e. the sentences of the language PL, to the integer objects.

For example, the sentence 4711 of the language denotes a semantic value which can be calculated using the function Φ:

$$\Phi\,[4711] \quad = 10 * \Phi\,[471] + \Phi\,[1]$$
$$= 10 * (10 * \Phi\,[47] + \Phi\,[1]) + \Phi\,[1]$$
$$= 10 * (10 * (10 * \Phi\,[4] + \Phi\,[7]) + \Phi\,[1]) + \Phi\,[1]$$
$$= 10 * (10 * (10 * 4 + 7) + 1) + 1$$
$$= 4711$$

The given example is very simple, but the reader should recognize the difference between a sentence 4711 and its semantic, which is represented by the abstract integer object 4711.

```
num   := 0;   symbol := numeral;

WHILE   ch IN Digits   DO
   digit := ORD(ch)  -  ORD('0');
   IF   num <= (MaxInt - digit) DIV 10   THEN
      num := num * 10  +  digit;
      readch (ch);
   ELSE
      num := 0;
      Error (…)   (* skip the remaining digits *)
   END;
END;
```

Fig. 9.1. Recognition of numerals in syntactic analysis of a compiler

Similar to that classical example we can define other semantic valuation functions representing a mapping from language elements to mathematical or logical objects which represent their meaning. Obviously, a complete system for the description of a language, such as ADA for example, can get rather complex. However, it is given in a clear formal way and it allows not only the definition of the semantics of a programming language, but it is also the foundation for proving the correctness of certain programs written in that language as well as proving correctness of the language's implementation. Moreover, semantic valuation functions can directly be used for the implementation of a language. This is shown in Figure 9.1, which shows a typical code fragment that can be found in the scanner of various compilers.

The code fragment of Figure 9.1 directly reflects the above introduced semantic valuation function Φ.

9.4   Axiomatic Semantics

Axiomatic semantics is also based on mathematical logic. The approach provides
rules of inference (the axioms) which show the change of data after the execution
of a certain sentence of the language. The typical situation is that the execution (i.e.
the transformation of data) takes place provided that the data satisfies certain
conditions, and the inference rules are used to deduce the results satisfying also
some conditions. Hoare introduced the following notation to describe what a program does [HOAR 69]:

    { P }   S   { Q }

where S is a program (or a part of a program) written in a certain programming language, and P and Q are logical expressions (assertions, using standard mathematical notations together with logical operators) describing conditions on the program
variables used in S. The meaning is "*If assertion P is true when control is at the
beginning of program S, then assertion Q will be true when control is at the end of
program S.*" The language of the assertions is predicate logic, the logical expressions P and Q are called predicates. Considering the transformation of predicates
leads to axiomatic semantics. The basic ideas were suggested by Floyd [FLOY 67]
and have been developed by Hoare [HOAR 69].

A simple example can be given in the following way, where we assume a and b to
be integers:

    { b > 10 }   a :=   10 + 4*b   { a > 20 }

meaning that if b > 10 before executing the assignment a := 10 + 4*b, then
the value of a will be greater 20 after the assignment is executed. Another example
could be:

    { X=x ∧ Y=y } BEGIN R := X;X := Y;Y := R END { X=y ∧ Y=x }

This means, that if the value of X is x and the value of Y is y before the initiation of
BEGIN R := X;X := Y;Y := R END, then the value of X will be y and the value
of Y will be x (i.e. the values of X and Y are exchanged) on completion of the program. The predicates P and Q are called *precondition* and *postcondition*, respectively.

Especially the first of the two given examples shows that we can have several preconditions for a given statement and a given postcondition; other valid preconditions for this example are

    { b > 3 }, { b > 15 }, { b > 20 }, { b > 80 },   ...

Each of those precondition guarantees the postcondition for the given assignment statement, but only the first (i.e. { b > 3 }) is that precondition which is the least restrictive one.

While Hoare introduced only sufficient conditions with his formalism, Dijkstra introduced a more precise form with the least restrictive conditions which are sufficient and necessary [DIJK 75]. This least restrictive precondition is called *weakest precondition*, and is written as *wp(S, Q)*. Dijkstra calls the rules that describe wp *predicate transformer*. Thus, Hoare's notation can be replaced by

```
{ wp(S, Q) }    S    { Q }
```

Obviously, whenever a precondition holds, the weakest precondition also holds. This statement holds, because any arbitrary precondition is more restrictive than the weakest precondition and, thus, is covered by the weakest precondition. This can be seen in our example.

The calculation of the weakest precondition is not always as obvious and simple as it might be implied by the above given example. More complex actions, such as WHILE control structures, for example, cause more problems in describing the predicate transformer. However, to give the reader the idea on how axiomatic semantics will work, in the following we introduce the predicate transformer for assignment statements, which is very simple. The assignment

```
x := expr
```

and the postcondition Q (x) have the weakest precondition

```
wp ( x := expr, Q (x) )    =    Q (expr)
```

Thus, the weakest precondition for an assignment is simply calculated by substituting any occurrence of x in the postcondition Q by the expression expr. For example, considering the above given assignment statement again:

```
a := 10 + 4*b
```

together with the postcondition Q:

```
{ a > 20 }
```

then, we calculate the weakest precondition by substituting 10 + 4*b for a in Q to get

```
10 + 4*b  >  20          ⇔
     4*b  >  20 - 10      ⇔
       b  >  10/4
```

Because b was in the given example assumed to be an integer, the weakest pre-condition

    { b > 3 }

holds.

Obviously, the handling of a sequence of (assignment) statements is easy, i.e. the predicate transformer for a statement sequence S1; S2 is given as

    wp (S1; S2, Q) = wp (S1, wp (S2, Q)) .

This means, the weakest precondition for the statement sequence S1; S2 and the postcondition Q is given by the weakest precondition of statement S1 and the corresponding postcondition, which is the weakest precondition for statement S2 and the postcondition Q.

The semantics of a programming language can be described, by having a predicate transformer for each language construct. Then, the predicate transformer characterizes in an exact way the transformation of the precondition of each basic construct of the programming language onto its postcondition (Note: if the weakest precondition is not satisfied, the postcondition cannot possible be satisfied). Therefore, the effect of any statement, or statement sequence (i.e. any program) can be described and, thus, the language's semantics is specified in a formal way.

Exercises

(1) Design three regular grammars which generate

    (a)   PASCAL names;
    (b)   odd numbers;
    (c)   the language $L = \{\, s^n \mid s \in \{01, 10\} \wedge n > 0 \,\}$.

Check the correctness of the production set.

(2) Let the language L be defined as $L = \{\, 0^n 1^{n-1} \mid n \geq 1 \,\}$. E.g., 0, 001, and 00011 are elements of L. Design a context-free grammar G (T, N, P, S) which generates L and where $|N| = 1$ and $|P| = 2$.

(3) Given the ambiguous grammar G (T, N, P, S):

    T : $\{0, 1\}$
    N : $\{A, B\}$
    P :   A $\rightarrow$ 0BB
             B $\rightarrow$ 1A | 0A | 0
    S :   A

Show for a suitable word the different syntax trees (parse trees).

(4) Proof that LL(1)-grammars
    a)   are unambiguous,
    b)   can never be left recursive.

(5) What are the differences between PASCAL's type definition facilities and abstract data types?

(6) Strong typing:

- What does it mean?

- What are the advantages?

- Give a simple example which shows that PASCAL, as defined in the Jensen/Wirth report is not strongly typed.

(7) Explain the pros and cons of representing Boolean values as a single bit in memory.

(8) Choose two high level programming languages and contrast their definitions of the array data type.

(9) PASCAL provides *file* and *set* types. Describe the data objects of these two types and the appropriate set of operations.

(10) Multidimensional arrays can be stored in row-major form (e.g. in PASCAL) or in column-major form (e.g. in FORTRAN). Develop the access functions for both forms for 3-dimensional arrays.

(11) Why is the cardinality of sets in PASCAL implementations usually restricted? What are the advantages/disadvantages?

(12) Arrays and records are both aggregates of data. What are the differences? On which mathematical concepts are they based?

(13) In PASCAL or MODULA-2, a pointer can only reference objects of a certain type; in PL/1, a pointer can reference objects of any type. What are the effects of these two different concepts?

(14) Why is it impossible to allocate memory statically for recursively defined data structures?

(15) What does dereferencing mean? Give an example.

(16) An example that PASCAL (according to the Jensen/Wirth report) is not strongly typed is that the type of a procedure parameter cannot be determined at compile time. Which feature of MODULA-2 solves this problem? Explain.

(17) Discuss problems with the evaluation of boolean expressions.

(18) What is the difference between counter-decided and condition-decided control structures?

(19) Given the following SIMULA 67 program fragment. List scope and lifetime of the declared variables in a table.

```
BEGIN
      REAL   X, Y;
      INTEGER   I, J, K, N;
            statements
      BEGIN
            REAL   X1, N;
            INTEGER   A, J;
                  statements
            BEGIN
                  REAL   X;
                  INTEGER   A, K, N;
                        statements
            END;
            statements
            BEGIN
                  REAL   A, B, N;
                  INTEGER   H, I;
                        statements
            END;
            statements
      END;
            statements
END;
```

(20) Given the following PASCAL program. What is the output? Explain.

```
program iftest (input, output);
var  e1, e2: boolean;
begin
  e2 := true;
  e1 := false;
  if e1 then
    if e2 then
      writeln('one')
  else
    writeln('two');
  if e1 then
```

```
        begin
          if e2 then
            writeln ('three')
        end
        else writeln('four');
      end.
```

(21) Discuss the different parameter passing methods. What are the advantages and disadvantages?

(22) Given the following PASCAL-like program fragment:

```
program prog;
      procedure proc1;
            procedure proc2;

                  ...

                  proc1;

                  ...

            end;

            ...

            proc2;

            ...

      end;
      procedure proc3;

            ...

            proc1;

            ...

      end;

      ...

      proc3;

      ...

end;
```

Describe each stage in the life of the stack until proc1 is called in procedure proc2. Show the dynamic and static links after each procedure call.

(23) Concerning overloading of operators and procedures, are there differences from a compiler writer's point of view? Explain.

(24) Compare the concept of overloaded procedures and generic procedures. Give an example program for both concepts in ADA.

(25) Discuss abstract data types in terms of abstraction, information hiding and encapsulation (what do these terms mean?). Which features must be provided by a programming language to allow the definition and usage of abstract data types?

(26) Does SIMULA 67 provide abstract data types? If YES, give an example. If NO, explain why.

(27) Compare classes in SIMULA 67, EIFFEL, and C++.

(28) Compare the facilities to define abstract data types in MODULA-2 and ADA. What are the major differences?
Give an example for the definition and usage of an abstract data type in both, MODULA-2 and ADA.

(29) What does *dangling reference* stand for?
Give a PL/1 program fragment to generate a dangling reference.

(30) a)   Explain the concept of strong typing.
b)   Consider PASCAL as introduced in the Jensen/Wirth report. Is PASCAL a strongly typed language. Give two examples to verify your answer and explain them.
c)   What about strong typing of MODULA-2? Consider your examples from b) and explain.

(31) a)   Explain Dijkstra's *guarded commands* for selection statements. What is the most interesting point in terms of overspecifying?
b)   How can the concept be expanded to be used for DO-loops?

(32) Assume a programming language in which all parameters are passed by reference. What are the advantages and disadvantages of this approach?

(33) a)   Multidimensional arrays are stored in an one dimensional way. Develop the formula to calculate the address of a certain array element $a[i_1, i_2, ..., i_k]$ of an array defined as a: array $[l_1..u_1, l_2..u_2, ..., l_k..u_k]$ of type. Assume the base address to be b_a and that the array is stored in row-major form.
b)   Give a PASCAL program fragment describing the algorithm to calculate the address of a certain array element of an array of arbitrary dimension k.

(34) Consider the queue problem as introduced in Chapter 6.
Define abstract data types for a stack in the style of the QADT data type in SIMULA 67, EIFFEL, C++, MODULA-2, and ADA.

(35) The following part of a grammar shows a well-known ambiguity problem in programming languages:

stmt → IF *expr* THEN *stmt* | IF *expr* THEN *stmt* ELSE *stmt* | *other*.

a) What is the problem?
b) How would you change the syntax of the language to overcome the problem (no semantic solutions!) ?
c) Formalize your suggestions of b) by replacing the above given grammar by a new one.

(36) a) Explain the paradigm of object-oriented programming.
b) What are the differences between extended types in OBERON and the class concept in SIMULA 67 in terms of inheritance?
c) Consider the following SMALLTALK example:

```
class name                    A
    instance variable names
    methods
        gamma
            self  delta
        delta
            printString 'ONE'


class name                    B
    superclass                A
    instance variable names
    methods
        delta
            printString 'TWO'
```

Assume x to be an instantiation of class B. What is the output by sending message **gamma** to x?

(37) Opaque types in MODULA-2 are restricted to pointer types (according to the 3rd edition of Wirth's book "Programming in MODULA-2").

a) Give an example to proof the necessity of this restriction in MODULA-2.
b) What are the advantages and disadvantages of this restriction?
c) Propose a way to hide a type's representation with no restrictions. Discuss the advantages and disadvantages. Has your approach already been introduced in another programming language? If yes, which one?

(38) Suppose a programming language allows the concurrent execution of program units and, therefore, provides a data type SEMAPHORE.

a) Describe the operations that can be performed on variables of this
type using a PASCAL-like pseudo code.

b) How would you actually implement those operations? Support your
assertion.

(39) The message passing concept for concurrent processes is based on Brinch
Hansen's *distributed processes* (DP) and Hoare's *communicating sequential
processes* (CSP).

a) Give an explanation on how DP and CSP handle nondeterminism.

b) Explain the differences between DP and CSP.

c) Use CSP to implement an integer semaphore, S, shared among an
array X(i:1..100) of client processes. Each process may increment the
semaphore by S!V() or decrement it by S!P(). The latter command
must be delayed if the value of the semaphore is not positive.

(40) a) Procedures are usually implemented using a stack and activation
records. Describe the typical elements of an activation record.

b) Consider the following PASCAL program fragment.

```
program alpha;
var  x : integer;
    procedure p1;
    var  x1, x2, x3 : integer;
        procedure p2;
        var x1, x4 : integer;
        begin
→           x1 := x2 + x;
        end;
        procedure p3;
        var x2, x5 : integer;
            procedure p4;
            var x3, x5 : integer;
            begin
                ...  p2;   ...
            end;
        begin
            ...  p4;   ...
        end;
    begin
```

```
            ...    p3;   ...
          end;
        begin (*main*)
            ...   p1;   ...
        end.
```

Describe each stage in the life of the stack until procedure p2 is called and executed. Show the dynamic and static links after each procedure call.

c) Explain the access of the variables of the marked statement in procedure p2 in terms of dynamic and/or static links.

(41) Consider procedures in ADA.

a) ADA knows two forms of binding between actual and formal parameters. Describe both of them! Do you think that both forms are necessary? Support your assertion.

b) Describe the differences in the concepts between ADA's overloaded procedures and generic procedures.

(42) a) Consider procedure parameters in PASCAL. Are there differences between their introduction in the original Jensen/Wirth report and in the ISO standard? If yes, what are the reasons. If no, how are PASCAL's procedure parameters reflected in MODULA-2?

b) Consider the following program fragment given in some pseudo code:

```
...
var  i : integer;
     a : array [1..2] of integer;
...
procedure swap (mode x, y: integer);
var  z : integer;
begin
   z := x;
   x := y;
   y := z;
end swap;
...
i := 1;
a[1] := 2;
a[2] := 3;
swap (i,a[i]);
writeln(i,' ',a[1],' ',a[2]);
...
```

What is the output, if the parameters are passed by

i)   value,
ii)   reference,
iii)   value-result,
iv)   result, or by
v)   name?

(43) What do we mean by reference count? Give an example!

(44) Discuss and compare the selection and repetition statements of the following programming languages: FORTRAN, ALGOL-68, PASCAL, C, and MODULA-2.

(45) Compute the weakest precondition for the following statements and post-conditions:

```
a)    x  :=  2 * (y - 1) - 1    { x > 0 }
      b)    h  :=  x + 2  -  x * 2    { h > 10 }
      c)    a  :=  4 * b + 2;
            b  :=  a/2 - 5;
            { b < 0 }
```

References

[ACM 78]   1977 ACM Turing Award, *CACM* **21**, p. 613 (1978).

[ACM 81]   1980 ACM Turing Award, *CACM* **24**, p. 75 (1981).

[ACM 85]   1984 ACM Turing Award, *CACM* **28**, p. 159 (1978).

[ADA 79]   Part A: Preliminary ADA Reference Manual. Part B: Rationale for the Design of the ADA Programming Language. *ACM SIGPLAN Notices* **14** (1979).

[AHOS 86]   A. V. Aho, R. Sethi, J. D. Ullman. *Compilers - Principles, Techniques and Tools*. Addison-Wesley, Reading (1986).

[ALLI 86]   L. Allison. *A Practical Introduction to Denotational Semantics*. Cambridge University Press, Cambridge (1986).

[ANDR 83]   G. R. Andrews, F. B. Schneider. Concepts and Notations for Concurrent Programming. *Computing Surveys* **15**, 3 - 43 (1983).

[BACK 57]   J. W. Backus, et al. The Fortran Automatic Coding System. *Proc. Western Joint Computer Conference*, Los Angeles (1957), 188 - 198. Reprinted in S. Rosen. *Programming Systems and Languages*. McGraw Hill, New York (1967).

[BACK 78]   J. Backus. Can Programming Be Liberated from the von Neumann Style? A Functional Style and Its Algebra of Programs. ACM Turing Award Lecture, *CACM* **21**, 613 - 641 (1978).

[BARN 89]   J. G. P. Barnes. *Programming in ADA. Third Edition*. Addison-Wesley, Reading (1989).

[BIRT 73]   G. M. Birtwistle, O. Dahl, B. Myhrhaug, K. Nygaard. *SIMULA BEGIN*. Petrocelli, New York (1973).

[BOHL 81]   G. Bohlender, K. Grüner, E. Kaucher, R. Klatte, W. Krämer, U. W. Kulisch, S. M. Rump, C. Ullrich, J. Wolff von Gudenberg, W. L. Miranker. *PASCAL-SC: A PASCAL for Contemporary Scientific Computation.* Research Report RC 9009, IBM T. J. Watson Research Center, Yorktown Heights (1981).

[BOWL 79]   K. L. Bowles. *Beginner's Manual for the UCSD PASCAL System.* Byte Books (McGraw Hill), Peterborough (1979).

[BRIN 73]   P. Brinch Hansen. *Operating System Principles.* Prentice Hall, Englewood Cliffs (1973).

[BRIN 75a]   P. Brinch Hansen. *CONCURRENT PASCAL Report.* Information Science, California Institute of Technology, Pasadena (1975).

[BRIN 75b]   P. Brinch Hansen. *CONCURRENT PASCAL Introduction.* Information Science, California Institute of Technology, Pasadena (1975).

[BRIN 78]   P. Brinch Hansen. Distributed Processes: A Concurrent Programming Concept. *CACM* **21**(11), 934 - 941 (1978).

[BUST 78]   D. W. Bustard. *PASCAL PLUS Users Manual.* Report, Queen's University of Belfast (1978).

[BYRN 91]   W. E. Byrne. *Software Design Techniques for Large ADA Systems.* Digital Press, Bedford (1991).

[CHRI 86]   S. Christodoulakis et al. Multimedia Document Presentation, Information Extraction, and Document Formation in MINOS: A Model and a System. *ACM Trans. on Office Information Systems* **4**(4), (1986).

[CHUR 41]   A. Church. *The Calculi of λ-Conversion.* Annals of Mathematical Studies 6, Princeton University Press, Princeton (1941).

[CLOC 81]   W. F. Clocksin, C. S. Mellish. *Programming in PROLOG.* Springer-Verlag, Berlin (1981).

[COBO 74]   *American National Standard Programming Language COBOL.* ANSI X3.23-1974, American National Standards Institute, New York (1974).

[COOK 89]   S. Cook. (ed.). *Proceedings of the 1989 European Conference on Object-Oriented Programming.* Cambridge University Press (1989).

[DAHL 66]   O. J. Dahl, K. Nygaard. SIMULA - An ALGOL-Based Simulation Language. *CACM* **9**, 671 - 678 (1966).

[DIJK 68a]   E. W. Dijkstra. The Structure of THE Multiprogramming System. *CACM* **11**(5), 341 - 346 (1968).

[DIJK 68b]   E. W. Dijkstra. Co-operating Sequential Processes. In: F. Genuys (ed.): *Programming Languages.* Academic Press, London (1968).

[DIJK 72]   E. W. Dijkstra. The Humble Programmer. ACM Turing Award Lecture, *CACM* **15**, 859 - 866 (1972).

[DIJK 75]   E. W. Dijkstra. Guarded Commands, Nondeterminancy, and Formal Derivation of Programs. *CACM* **18**, 453 - 457 (1975).

[FARB 64]   D. J. Farber, R. E. Griswold, I. P. Polonsky. SNOBOL - A String Manipulation Language. *Journal of the ACM* **11**, 21 - 30 (1964).

[FISC 88]   C. N. Fischer and R. J. LeBlanc. *Crafting a Compiler.* Benjamin/Cummings Publishing, Menlo Park (1988).

[FLOY 67]   R. W. Floyd. Assigning Meanings to Programs. In: J. T. Schwartz (ed.). *Mathematical Aspects of Computer Science, Proceedings of Symposia in Applied Mathematics 19*, Providence (1967).

[FORT 66]   *United States of America Standard FORTRAN.* USAS X3.9-1966, United States of America Standards Institute, New York (1966).

[FORT 78]   *American National Standard Programming Language FORTRAN.* ANSI X3.9-1978, American National Standards Institute, New York (1978).

[GHEZ 82]   C. Ghezzi, M. Jazayeri. *Programming Language Concepts.* John Wiley & Sons, New York (1982).

[GIAN 86]   F. Giannesini, H. Kanoui, R. Pasero, M. van Caneghem. *PROLOG.* Addison-Wesley, Reading (1986).

[GOLD 83]   A. Goldberg, D. Robson. *SMALLTALK-80: The Language and its Implementation.* Addison-Wesley, Reading (1983).

[GRIS 71]   R. E. Grieswold, J. F. Poage, I. P. Polonsky. *The SNOBOL4 Programming Language.* Prentice Hall, Englewood Cliffs (1971).

[GUTK 84]   J. Gutknecht. Tutorial on MODULA-2. *BYTE* **9**(8), (1984).

[HEXT 90]   J. Hext. *Programming Structures, Vol. 1.* Prentice Hall, Sydney
                (1990).

[HOAR 69]   C. A. R. Hoare. An Axiomatic Basis for Computer Programming.
                CACM **12**(10), 576 - 580 (1969).

[HOAR 74]   C. A. R. Hoare. Monitors: An Operating System Structuring Concept.
                CACM **17**(10), 238 - 250 (1974).

[HOAR 78]   C. A. R. Hoare. Communicating Sequential Processes. *CACM*
                21(8), 666 - 677 (1978).

[HOAR 81]   C. A. R. Hoare. The Emperor's Old Clothes. ACM Turing Award
                Lecture, *CACM* **24**, 75 - 83 (1981).

[HOAR 90]   C. A. R. Hoare. (ed.). *Developments in Concurrency and
                Communication.* Addison-Wesley, Reading (1990).

[HORO 84]   E. Horowitz. *Fundamentals of Programming Languages.* Springer-
                Verlag, Berlin (1984).

[IEEE 82]   IEEE Computer Society. *A Proposed Standard for Binary Floating-
                point Arithmetic.* Draft 10.0, IEEE Task P754 (1982).

[INGA 81]   D. H. H. Ingalls. Design Principles Behind SMALLTALK. *BYTE* **6**,
                286 - 298 (August 1981).

[IVER 62]   K. E. Iverson. *A Programming Language.* John Wiley & Sons, New
                York (1962).

[JENS 74]   K. Jensen, N. Wirth. *Pascal User Manual and Report.* Springer-
                Verlag, Berlin (1974).

[JONE 90]   R. Jones, C. Maynard, I. Stuart. *The Art of LISP Programming.*
                Springer-Verlag, Berlin (1990).

[KAEH 86]   T. Kaehler, D. Patterson. A Small Taste of SMALLTALK. *BYTE* **11**,
                145 - 159 (August 1986).

[KAMI 90]   S. N. Kamin. *Programming Languages.* Addison-Wesley, Reading
                (1990).

[KERN 78]   B. W. Kernighan, D. M. Ritchie. *The C Programming Language.*
                Prentice Hall, Englewood Cliffs (1978).

[KERN 88]   B. W. Kernighan, D. M. Ritchie. *The C Programming Language.*
                Second Edition. Prentice Hall, Englewood Cliffs (1988).

[KUIC 86]   W. Kuich, A. Salomaa. *Semirings, Automata, Languages.* Springer-Verlag, Berlin (1986).

[KULI 81]   U. Kulisch, W. Miranker. *Computer Arithmetic in Theory and Practice.* Academic Press, New York (1981).

[LISK 81]   B. Liskow. *CLU Reference Manual.* Springer-Verlag, Berlin (1981).

[MART 86]   J. Martin. *Fourth Generation Languages, Vol. I - Vol. III.* Prentice Hall, Englewood Cliffs (1986).

[MATO 89]   V. M. Matos, P. J. Jalics. An Experimental Analysis of the Performance of Fourth Generation Tools on PCs. *CACM 32*, 1340 - 1351 (1989).

[MCCA 60]   J. McCarthy. Recursive Functions of Symbolic Expressions and Their Computation by Machine. *CACM 3*, 184 - 195 (1960).

[MCCA 65]   J. McCarthy, P. W. Abrahams, D. J. Edwards, T. P. Hart, M.I.Levin. *LISP 1.5 Programmer's Manual.* MIT Press, Cambridge (1965).

[METC 87]   M. Metcalf, J. K. Reid. *FORTRAN 8X Explained.* Oxford University Press, New York (1987).

[MEYE 87]   B. Meyer. EIFFEL: Programming for Reusability and Extendibility. *SIGPLAN Notices*, Vol. **22**, No. 2, 1987.

[MEYE 88]   B. Meyer. *Object-oriented Software Construction.* Prentice Hall, Englewood Cliffs, 1988.

[MEYE 90]   B. Meyer. *EIFFEL: The Language.* Prentice Hall, Englewood Cliffs, 1990.

[MITC 79]   J. G. Mitchell, W. Maybury, R. Sweet. *Mesa Language Manual.* Technical Report CSL-78-1, Xerox PARC, Palo Alto (1979).

[NAUR 63]   P. Naur (ed.). Revised Report on the Algorithmic Language ALGOL 60. *CACM 6* (1963), 1 - 17; *Comp. J.* **5** (1962/63), 349 - 367; *Num. Math.* **4** (1963), 420 - 453.

[PARN 71]   D. L. Parnas. Information Distribution Aspects of Design Methodology.. *Proc. IFIP Congress 71*, 339 - 344 (1971).

[PARN 72]   D. L. Parnas. On the Criteria to be Used in Decomposing Systems into Modules. *CACM 15*, 1053 - 1058 (1972).

[PL/1 76]   *American National Standard Programming Language PL/1.* ANSI
               X3.53-1976, American National Standards Institute, New York
               (1976).

[PRAT 84]   T. W. Pratt. *Programming Languages: Design and Implementation.*
               2nd Ed. Prentice-Hall, Englewood Cliffs (1984).

[RICH 69]   M. Richards. BCPL: A Tool for Compiler Writing and Systems
               Programming. *AFIPS Conference Proceedings,* 557 - 566 (1969).

[SALO 73]   A. K. Salomaa. *Formal Languages.* Academic Press, New York
               (1973).

[SAMM 69]   J. E. Sammet. *Programming Languages: History and Fundamen-*
               tals. Prentice-Hall, Englewood Cliffs (1969).

[SCHM 80]   J. W. Schmidt, M. Mall. *PASCAL/R Report.* Report No. 66,
               Fachbereich Informatik, Universität Hamburg (1980).

[SCOT 70]   D. Scott. Outline of a Mathematical Theory of Computation. *Proc 4th*
               Princeton Conf. on Information Sci. and Syst. (1970).

[SCOT 71]   D. Scott, C. Strachey. Towards a mathematical semantics for com-
               puter languages. *Proc. Symp. on Computers and Automata,*
               Polytechnic Inst. of Brooklyn (1971).

[SEBE 89]   R. W. Sebesta. *Concepts of Programming Languages.*
               Benjamin/Cummings, Redwood City (1989).

[SETH 89]   R. Sethi. *Programming Languages.* Addison-Wesley, Reading
               (1989).

[SHAF 91]   D. Shafer, D. A. Ritz. *Practical SMALLTALK.* Springer-Verlag, Berlin
               (1991).

[SILB 88]   A. Silberschatz, J. Peterson. *Operating Systems Concepts.*
               Addison-Wesley, Reading (1988).

[SMIT 90]   J. D. Smith. *Reusability and Software Construction: C and C++.*
               John Wiley & Sons, New York (1990).

[STER 90]   L. S. Sterling. (ed.). *The Practice of Prolog.* MIT Press, Cambridge
               (1990).

[STRO 86]   B. Stroustrup. *The C++ Programming Language.* Addison-Wesley,
               Reading (1986).

[TEUF 84]   T. Teufel. *Ein optimaler Gleitkommaprozessor*. Dissertation, Universität Karlsruhe, Karlsruhe (1984).

[TEUF 89]   B. Teufel. *Compilers*. Notes CSCI333, Department of Computing Science, The University of Wollongong (1989).

[TORB 91]   B. J. Torby. *Fortran 77 for Engineers*. Prentice Hall, Englewood Cliffs (1991).

[VANW 69]   A. van Wijngaarden, B. J. Mailloux, J. E. L. Peck, C. H. A. Koster. Report of the Algorithmic Language ALGOL 68. *Numerische Mathematik* **14**, 79 - 218 (1969).

[WAIT 84]   W. Waite, G. Goos. *Compiler Construction*. Springer-Verlag, New York (1984).

[WEGN 72]   P. Wegner. The Vienna Definition Language. *Computing Surveys* **4**, 5 - 63, 1972

[WIRT 66a]   N. Wirth, C. A. R. Hoare. A Contribution to the Development of ALGOL. *CACM* **9**, 413 - 431 (1966).

[WIRT 66b]   N. Wirth, H. Weber. EULER: A Generalization of ALGOL and its Formal Definition. *CACM* **9**, 13 - 23 and 89 - 99 (1966).

[WIRT 71a]   N. Wirth. The Programming Language PASCAL. *Acta Informatica* **1**, 35 - 63 (1971).

[WIRT 71b]   N. Wirth. Program Development by Stepwise Refinement. *CACM* **14**(4), 221 - 227 (1971).

[WIRT 74]   N. Wirth. On the Composition of Well-structured Programs. *Computing Surveys* **6**(4), 247 - 259 (1974).

[WIRT 76]   N. Wirth. *Algorithms + Data Structures = Programs*. Prentice-Hall, Englewood Cliffs (1976).

[WIRT 78]   N. Wirth. *MODULA-2*. Report No. 27, Institut für Informatik, ETH Zürich (1978).

[WIRT 81]   N. Wirth. *Compilerbau*. B. G. Teubner, Stuttgart (1981).

[WIRT 85]   N. Wirth. From Programming Language Design to Computer Construction. ACM Turing Award Lecture, *CACM* **28**, 159 - 164 (1985).

[WIRT 88a]   N. Wirth. *Programming in MODULA-2, Fourth Edition.* Springer-
               Verlag, Berlin (1988).

[WIRT 88b]   N. Wirth. From MODULA to OBERON. *Software - Practice and
               Experience* **18**, 661 - 670 (1988).

[WIRT 88c]   N. Wirth. The Programming Language OBERON. *Software -
               Practice and Experience* **18**, 671 - 690 (1988).

[WIRT 88d]   N. Wirth. Type Extensions. *ACM Trans. on Prog. Lang. and Syst.*
               10, 204 - 214 (1988).

[WIRT 90]   N. Wirth. *From MODULA to OBERON: the Programming Language
               OBERON.* Report No. 143, Department Informatik, ETH Zürich
               (1990).

[XERO 81]   The Xerox Learning Research Group. The SMALLTALK-80 System.
               BYTE **6**, 36 - 48 (August 1981).

Index

New by Springer-Verlag

Dimitris Karagiannis (ed.)

Database and Expert Systems Applications

Proceedings of the International Conference in Berlin,
Federal Republic of Germany, 1991

1991. 351 figures. XIV, 570 pages.
Soft cover DM 148,–, öS 1036,–
ISBN 3-211-82301-8

Use and development of database and expert systems can be found in
all fields of computer science. The aim of this book is to present a large
spectrum of already implemented or just being developed database and
expert systems.
Contributions cover new requirements, concepts for implementations
(e.g. languages, models, storage structures), management of meta data,
system architectures, and experiences gained by using traditional databases in as many areas of applications as possible.
The aim of the book is to inspire a fruitful dialogue between development in practice, users of database and expert systems, and scientists
working in the field.

Springer-Verlag Wien New York

Sachsenplatz 4–6, P.O. Box 89, A-1201 Wien · Heidelberger Platz 3, D-1000 Berlin 33
175 Fifth Avenue, New York, NY 10010, USA · 37-3, Hongo 3-chome, Bunkyo-ku, Tokyo 113, Japan

SpringerWienNewYork